The Subversive Bible

The Subversive Bible

Jonathan Magonet

SCM PRESS LTD

0 334 02671 7

First published in Britain 1997
by SCM Press Ltd
9–17 St Albans Place, London N1 0N X

Typeset at The Spartan Press Ltd
Lymington, Hants
and printed in Great Britain by
Biddles Ltd, Guildford and King's Lynn.

Dedicated to the memory of
Anneliese Debray
Gisela Hommel
Dr Charlotte Klein
Alisa Stadler

For Doro, Gav and Avi
with all my love

Contents

Preface

This book began with a great title, *The Subversive Bible*. But though it seemed an easy task at first to pull together appropriate themes and materials, it took much longer than I had assumed. Part of the reason lay in the realization that with three books on the Hebrew Bible behind me, there was a risk of repeating myself – a common enough failing but still a great sin. So a lot more pruning was needed, and rethinking, than I had originally anticipated.

Then I remembered another long-cherished wish – to put into book form some of the sermons delivered over the years at the Hedwig Dransfeld Haus, Bendorf, Germany, during the annual Jewish–Christian Bible Week and the Jewish–Christian–Muslim Student Conference. But how to justify their inclusion in a book on this subject? Sermons, at least good ones, can translate biblical ideas into the life of a community, so they could complement the more analytical chapters in the first part of the book. Unfortunately sermons are a 'turn-off' for many. Nevertheless these did have an impact in their original context and I hope that they will appeal. (Not all of them will be recognizable as sermons in any classical sense, if that is any encouragement to read on.)

The two sections are linked by a chapter (6) that stands alone. Between the Bible itself and the community to which it belongs is the reader, whether a private individual, a scholar or cleric. But each reader brings a whole range of assumptions and presuppositions to the task. These are often unconscious and rarely declared. So this particular chapter is an experiment at exposing some of the issues this raises. For if the Bible is sometimes subversive, it is all too often subverted in turn by its interpreters. Today we know that we have to interpret those who interpret the text on our behalf.

Which effectively brings me back to this reader and writer who is also selling you a particular line. So please treat this book, too, with all the critical questioning you can muster.

As usual this book owes much to others: the patience of my wife Dorothea and my children Gavriel and Avigail; the support of Ute Stamm of the Hedwig Dransfeld Haus who has maintained the Bendorf end of these interfaith conferences for so many years; friends, colleagues and students with whom I have tried out the ideas presented here in various forms; John Bowden who continues to produce an exciting and varied list for SCM Press, including a growing number of Rabbinic authors; the Leo Baeck College, currently celebrating its fortieth anniversary, for the opportunities it has given me over so many years to learn and teach – and disappear from time to time to foreign parts.

It is a particular pleasure to include on the front cover a detail of a painting by my grandfather Julius Slonims. I never knew him but feel a great affinity with him. He was reputedly a Talmudic scholar and founded the orthodox 'Federation Synagogue' in Clapton. Yet he was clearly a 'modern' man, writing stories in Hebrew, and a gifted artist. The cover picture is actually a copy he made of a once celebrated painting by the German Jewish artist Eduard Bendemann (1811–1889) of 'Jeremiah at the Destruction of Jerusalem'. It depicts brilliantly the disturbing power of prophecy and the tragic role of the prophet. But where did my grandfather see it to paint it? The original seemingly remained in Germany which he never visited. However a black and white photo exists in the old Jewish Encyclopedia of 1903 at the front of Vol. 3. If he copied from that it is truly an extraordinary piece of work. He passed on his artistic talent to at least three generations, though my share was only an ability, long since unused, to do simple caricatures. Instead it was his love of Jewish learning that I inherited, and I hope he would have approved of his grandson, who is a very different kind of Rabbi in a very different kind of world.

Rabbi Professor Jonathan Magonet

1

The Subversive Bible

'It ain't necessarily so!'

In a way, the title says it all. The Hebrew Bible is subversive, even dangerous, and we take a risk when we read it. Perhaps it is enough to state that and leave it up to the reader to find the myriad examples that would confirm or challenge this statement. But all too often the Bible remains a talked about but unread book. So how open up its special world to a readership unfamiliar with its language, conventions and purposes?

At the risk of appearing sacriligious it has to be said that the Bible is not just a 'pious' document to be handled with kid gloves. To do so is to forget its wide sweep of concerns, its overarching humanity and its extraordinary power to move and challenge. To do so is also to forget that on some level it is 'folk literature' that in its origins spoke directly to people and has continued to do so in the more than two millennia since its completion. It met people where they were.

Its reputation stands in the way of our reading it afresh. Moreover we come to it in translation and this makes for difficulties for a variety of reasons. The classic translation of King James, though magnificent in its time and way, puts too many barriers between us and the directness of the biblical text. It makes it feel like an ancient document instead of a contemporary one. And some of the language is simply misleading today. 'Vanity of vanities', the opening of Ecclesiastes, does not mean 'vain' as we use it today but something 'insubstantial' which is closer to the Hebrew *'hevel'* which means 'a breath' or 'vapour'. Unfortunately some of the newer translations fall into the opposite trap. By oversimplifying or trying to catch a modern idiom they lose out on the subtleties and interconnections within the original Hebrew text. Things simply get lost.

Then there is the problem of who owns the Bible. Understandably we tend to encounter it in a religious context which colours our approach. And if we have problems with organized religion the Bible gets tossed out with the bathwater. Yet even a cursory glance at the Bible shows that it covers too many areas of human life and experience, is composed in too many different styles and modes, to fit very comfortably into conventional religious forms. Or to put it even more bluntly. We tend to dismiss the Bible on the basis of a few half-remembered childhood stories and the solemn way we usually hear it intoned, so we never even get near it or see its relevance. If Shakespeare had been read in the way that Bible texts are usually read he would never have got out of Stratford-on-Avon.

So this book is an invitation to take another look at the different materials to be found within the Bible, recognizing just how unconventional they are once freed of our prejudices against it.

Some may find the suggestion that the Bible is 'subversive' to be offensive, though there is no reason why they should. We have only to think of the activity of the prophets in attacking the powers-that-be, sometimes at the cost of their lives, to realize just how challenging the contents of the Bible can be. The prophets were subversive activists in their time, and by recording their words and deeds, the Bible effectively repeats their provocation in every subsequent generation.

That the Bible has been provocative is easily proven from the way in which so many different revolutionary movements have found their inspiration and justification in its pages – and the way in which those in power have sought to control its impact by their own system of interpretation or by simply preventing access to it.

The most obvious example of a biblical story which has inspired and fed revolutionary thought throughout the ages is the Exodus from Egypt. Its message is summed up in the familiar black spiritual:

When Israel was in Egypt's land
  Let My people go!
Oppressed so hard they could not stand
  Let My people go!
Go down, Moses, way down in Egypt's land
Tell old Pharaoh to let My people go!

In his classic study *Exodus and Revolution* the political

philosopher Michael Walzer explores the impact of the story of the Exodus on different liberation movements.

The escape from bondage, the wilderness journey, the Sinai covenant, the promised land: all these loom large in the literature of revolution. Indeed, revolution has often been imagined as an enactment of the Exodus and the Exodus has often been imagined as a program for revolution.

[The Exodus] is central to the communist theology or anti-theology of Ernst Bloch, the source and original of his 'principle of hope' . . . It is the subject of a book by Lincoln Steffens, called *Moses in Red*, published in 1926, a detailed account of Israel's political struggles in the wilderness and a defense of Leninist politics. It plays a large part in the 'liberation theology' worked out by Catholic priests in Latin America . . . It figures prominently in medieval debates over the legitimacy of crusading warfare. It is important to the political argument of the radical monk Savonarola, who preached twenty-two sermons on the Book of Exodus in the months just before his fall and execution. It is cited in the pamphlets of the German peasants' revolt. John Calvin and John Knox justified their most extreme political positions by quoting from Exodus. The text underpins the radical contractualism of the Huguenot *Vindiciae Contra Tyrannos* and then of the Scottish Presbyterians. It is crucial . . . to the self-understanding of the English Puritans during the 1640s, and of the Americans, too, on their 'errand into the wilderness'. It is an important source of both argument and symbolism during the American Revolution and the establishment on these shores of 'God's new Israel'. . . . . The Book of Exodus came alive in the hands of Boer nationalists fighting the British, and it is alive in the hands of black nationalists in South Africa today.[1]

Perhaps it is necessary here to clarify which 'Bible' I am talking about. It is not the solemn black-bound volume to be found on shelves in churches or in hotel room drawers, the one containing the 'Old' and 'New' Testaments. My concern is the first part of that book, the 'Hebrew Bible' which ends a couple of centuries before the advent of Christianity and needs to be understood in its own time and place. It still takes up more than two-thirds of that 'black-bound' book but its origins are in another world and another

language and we need more than just a translation to understand
what it is about. That is an issue we will be addressing from time to
time as we examine the different subjects of this study. But the point
to make is simply that the Hebrew Bible is both the familiar volume
and something other and alien that needs to be addressed in its own
terms if we are to understand the challenges it presents to us. Its
power comes through in the translations, but its essence remains to
be sought in every generation.

Tragically today the Bible is too often seen as simply the property
of the 'religious', and its various ideas are consigned to the realm of
myth or superstition by those who are unimpressed by or hostile to
religious systems or communities. But the Hebrew Bible is too
serious a book to be left to the 'religious' alone and within the
religious worlds it is too often hijacked to serve narrow sectarian
interests. It deserves better treatment from both camps.

I do not want to get into definitions of what is 'subversive'. This
book is an exploration rather than a formal thesis, but it may be
helpful to think in terms of two aspects of the Bible's subversive
power – what we may call extrinsic and intrinsic ones. The former is
typically the prophetic attack on the policies of a king or on the
activities of his contemporary priests and prophets, or on the
people's practice of idolatry. These are situations where the Bible
itself openly addresses some aspect of Israelite society and calls a
recognizable group of people to account. The 'intrinsic' aspect has
more to do with the presuppositions with which the Hebrew Bible
operates and the way it views the world. By its very nature, by the
stand it takes against the conventions of its own world, it subverts
the power structures or gender definitions or religious presuppositions of its own times.

It has to be said that a general statement that 'the Bible is
subversive' raises a number of problems. The Hebrew Bible is a
library, not a single book, and it contains any amount of contrasting, not to say mutually contradictory, material. Nevertheless it
must have had sufficient unity in the mind of the compilers of the
canon to have wanted to put it together. The alternative option is
simply to treat it as a ragbag collection of materials salvaged from
one or other of the crises that affected biblical Israel. In which case
it would be not unlike a recent American Jewish prayerbook that
had some twenty or so alternative services for the Shabbat designed
to appeal to every conceivable taste. In his review one critic

remarked rather unkindly that it was 'a triumph of the bookbinder's art'!

So given some kind of unity, the very contrasts that lie within the Bible actually contribute to its subversive quality since the reader is forced to engage in the debate. The conventional wisdom of Proverbs is savaged by the bitter outpourings of Job and the rigorous analysis of Ecclesiastes; the obsessive details of the cultic arrangements in Leviticus are questioned, if not actually undermined, by the repeated prophetic critique of injustice masking itself behind public piety; '"I can't bear iniquity and solemn assembly" says God' (Isa. 1.13). Spiritual certainties stand alongside equally spiritual doubts in the pages of the Psalms. Laws about proper sexual behaviour stand in stark contrast to the actual practice of the most pious patriarchs and heroic kings, let alone the erotic power of the Song of Songs. Despite the repeated quest for peace, 'to the near and to the far', the pages of the Bible are stained with blood, shed all too often in the name of the God of peace. Nor can such paradoxes, or for that matter such violence, simply be dismissed as the result of a 'primitive' level of religiosity, either to be superseded by a new and better covenant or explained away and justified in terms of an uncultured ancient world. We have to start with the premise that the sophistication of the biblical writers then was no less than ours – otherwise we would not still be reading their literary remains with such fascination and personal commitment.

If there are things we reject because no amount of interpretation or explaining can really justify them, then there are others that we have to recognize have yet to be taken seriously or implemented in our own 'advanced' society. If debts were abolished as in the Jubilee year (Lev. 25) so that people could periodically get a fresh start; if we did indeed love our neighbour as ourselves (Lev. 19.18); if we did beat our swords into ploughshares and no longer trained for war (Isa. 2.4); if we could be a blessing to all the families of the earth (Gen. 12.3) – then the world would be a better place, and we would not even need the Bible.

To press the point further home – our duty to read the Bible 'critically', with open eyes, with questions, even with judgments on the values it is offering us, is itself one of its legacies, and perhaps the most subversive of all. From Deuteronomy's 'you shall not add to the word which I command you nor take from it' (4.2) to Ecclesiastes' 'of making many books there is no end', we are pulled into valuing and evaluating everything between the covers of the books of this library, and by direct extension, the books of our traditions and our societies, and the private books of our lives. 'The sayings of the wise are like goads' (Ecc. 12.11).

What holds the Hebrew Bible together, despite its diversity and inner contradictions, is one simple premise – the One God, Creator of the world. This recognition of an ultimate unity in the created universe is an astonishing assertion. Scholars may argue whether it is a late sophisticated development of an earlier polytheism or monolatry, or whether monotheism is a revolutionary leap into a totally new kind of consciousness. By the time we have the Hebrew Bible before us, the idea is fully formed and assumed, though, like some archaeological dig, it is possible to trace the fossilized remains of older, or at least different, views of the world within it.

The first chapter of Genesis not only assumes the One God, who stands outside nature, but, with masterly certainty, ignores and thus effectively destroys entire mythological systems. Though elsewhere in the Hebrew Bible, especially in more poetic passages, some kind of angelic entourage will appear, there are no gods, demigods or powers present beside God in these majestic acts of separation and differentiation. The sun and moon, worshipped in many ways in other cultures, are reduced to light bulbs, convenient markers set in the sky to show the passage of the day and the changing seasons. The terrible sea monsters of legend are simply toys to play with in the immense bathtub that is the ocean – at least that is how it is presented as appearing from God's detached perspective; the great struggle between the gods and the cosmic waters of Ancient Near Eastern mythology simply disappears without trace. And to crown it all, with an almost nonchalant gesture, the whole of natural time, the solar and lunar cycles, is subordinated to the regular pattern of six days for labour and one for rest. God's time is stamped upon the world.

The second premise is no less wondrous than the first, that this God is intimately related to one particular part of the creation, human beings. This is expressed in their very formation, 'in our form, after our likeness' (Gen. 1.26). Only here of all the acts of creation is God's decision expressed in other than a straight command. With the phrase 'let us make a human being...', is evidence of a moment's pause in this astonishing display of divine versatility. The stage is festooned with multicoloured scarves and flags of all nations. Now the conjurer pauses over the black satin bag and we wait with baited breath to see what emerges. The Rabbis debated with whom God might have been consulting with this 'let us' – angels who objected to humans being created at all or simply an internal dialogue. But the moment of reflection already indicates something of what is at stake here for God, though the reason remains eternally unknown and unknowable.

We can project on to this God of Genesis any 'image' we wish, for that, after all is the corollary of being created in God's 'image'. A force discovering its own creative powers? An artist exploring the palette? A childlike being making a playful gesture? A solemn, purposeful parent? Perhaps the God who is outside the universe creates a being through which to explore that universe from within, seeing it through its eyes, living vicariously through the experiences of these creatures. A God eager to set them free to do whatsoever their fancy dictates, yet still wishing to control and determine their behaviour. A God who knows all yet who is repeatedly disappointed at the actions of these creatures.

It is not long before the limits of their freedom are explored by the first human couple. The immediate impulse comes from the snake, but because God has actually set a limit on their freedom of action some form of rebellion is inevitable. This challenge to their freedom has to be met, and the very prohibition itself can be seen as God's way of testing and exploring the curiosity, courage and independence of this new creation.

Within a generation of the first act of independence and the leaving of the Garden of Eden, the first murder will be committed and soon the world will become so corrupted that God will wish to destroy it. When the new population that descends from Noah proves equally problematic, the option to destroy is no longer available to a God who has imposed a further limitation on the divine power.[2] Instead the experiment with humanity will take on a new form. One man will be chosen, Abram, tested until he conforms with God's wish for a particular kind of human being, and from him will arise a nation on its own land that is to be a model for the rest of humanity. But before that can happen certain experiences have to be undergone.

I have suggested that the biblical picture depicts a Creator-God who is also in a process of learning. If human beings have been given freedom of action, within the limitations of their human nature and the brevity of their life, God can only stand back and indirectly guide their path along the lines God might wish. God can command but the human beings are free to choose whether or not to obey. Thus the cycles of stories about Abraham and Jacob both have as their central theme a willful act by the main character which causes God's plans to go astray. In both cases the act is instigated by a woman, a wife or mother, though ironically their intention is actually to help fulfil what they see as God's purpose. Abraham should have waited for the birth of Isaac and not listened to Sarah's urgings and taken Hagar; Jacob would have received God's special blessing from Isaac – he had no need to obey Rebeccah and steal the wrong blessing from his brother Esau. (What he takes is simply a blessing for material prosperity. When he returns from exile and confronts his brother he hands him a whole range of gifts which he consciously refers to as a 'blessing' (Gen. 33.11)).

In both these cases a great detour is made before the heroes get back on the right path God has planned – Ishmael has to be sent away to make room for Isaac, the promised child, and Jacob has to experience twenty years of exile. God's will prevails, but only when the human actors recognize that they have missed their way and have taken the appropriate steps to return.

While the heroes of these stories are learning from such experiences, God is also discovering more and more about these humans the hard way. The next stage in God's discovery of how human beings act moves on to the larger stage of nations. Jacob's descendants go down to Egypt.

We tend to read the story of the Exodus from Egypt in rather limited ways. Either we concentrate on it as Israel's story – how from the experience of slavery God brought Israel out to freedom with great and mighty acts as a preface to Sinai and the entry into the promised land. Or else we generalize it, seeing how such an act of liberation has consequences for every people in a state of 'slavery', however we may wish to define that. In either case we somehow take for granted the 'happy end'. What chance does a Pharaoh have against the Sovereign of the universe who can call up a whole host of plagues with which to attack him. Of course the ending was not so certain for those who took part – Moses was reluctant from the beginning and the children of Israel were terrified at changing their *status quo*. For the biblical author the outcome is certain, and God is depicted as acting with majesterial authority and didactic purpose. But another element may be there as well at the outset.

For example, we read God's words to Moses at the start of his mission. 'I have surely seen the suffering of My people who are in Egypt and their cry because of their taskmasters I have heard, for I know their suffering...' (Ex. 3.7). We read these words as evidence of God's compassion for those who suffer. One Rabbinic teaching assumes that the period of slavery was to have been longer, but that God felt the need to intervene because things were so bad. It is not too far from this idea to suggest that God too has to learn to understand what suffering on this scale means to these human creatures. God's words are not merely meant to reassure Moses and the Israelites – they reflect a discovery by God of the pain that human beings inflict upon each other in the freedom that has been granted to them. God cannot remain unmoved and seemingly indifferent – God has seen, God has heard, now God understands and must intervene. It is as if an area of God's experience has been awakened by identifying with these creatures made in the divine image; the relationship of Creator and creature is two-way. Now God has once again to set aside the divine detachment and enter the arena.

Once again we can reverse the poles of this divine-human engagement. For measured against the eternity of God we gain a new perspective on our own transience. Ecclesiastes seems to have been expressing this paradox in his customary pithy, if not always clear, manner:

[God] made everything appropriate in its time, also, [God] set eternity in their hearts so that human beings could not find out what God had done from the beginning to the end (Ecc. 3.11).

We exist between two realities, the vagaries of our individual daily lives and the awareness of a 'before and after' to our own personal existence and beyond even that of some partly glimpsed transcendent reality. Most of the Bible seems to assume a divine plan that guides and directs the workings of the world, a plan glimpsed by human beings through divine revelation. Conversely the author of Ecclesiastes starts instead with the sum total of human wisdom, empirical observations of a troubled humanity, and his own experience, whether real or imagined, and moves from there towards attempting to understand the will and actions of 'God'.

It ain't what you do it's the way that you do it!

This distance between divine reality and human perception is expressed in many ways throughout the Hebrew Bible. The consequences of not understanding it are all too often tragic. The Rabbis assumed that if only Israel had got it right the Bible would simply have consisted of the Five Books of Moses and the Book of Joshua: the conquest of the land, happy end! But one-third of their Bible is made up prophetic writings that try to live with the human propensity to fail and create their own disastrous fate. The bleakness of this outlook is nevertheless undermined by the sheer richness of the story-telling, the engagement it demands of the reader and the complexity of the stories that come down to us. Surprisingly, though the underlying message is potentially tragic, the mode of illustrating it is all too often comedy, absurdity and irony. It is precisely that unexpected dimension that further subverts our perception of what we think the Bible is or ought to be.

Granted, there are few belly-laughs in the Bible. Hardly surprising given the Bible's religious significance and the solemnity with which it is all-too-often addressed. And yet . . . If all of human life is to be found within it, then humour must be there, and even the possibility of some good vulgar slapstick. Well there is one belly-laugh that is quite literally that. It is about an immensely fat king called Eglon. His story is found in the Book of Judges which is organized according to a standard formula: Israel sins, then God sends a nation to punish them, Israel repents, God sends a 'judge' or leader to defeat their enemies, there is peace for forty years during the lifetime of the judge, then Israel sins again and the cycle repeats itself. In this particular round God sends against Israel Eglon, King of Moab, under whose rule they suffer for eighteen years, paying him a tribute (Judg. 3.12–30). When Israel finally turns to God, a saviour is sent in the person of a left-handed leader called Ehud ben Gera. The story continues as follows:

So Ehud made for himself a sword with two edges, a cubit in length. He wore it on his right thigh under his clothes. He presented the tribute to Eglon, king of Moab. Now it happened that Eglon, king of Moab, was extremely fat. So when [Ehud] had finished presenting the tribute, he sent away the people that carried the tribute. But then he turned back from the sculptured stones which were in Gilgal and said, 'I have a secret matter for you, O King.' He replied 'Silence!', and all the courtiers went out from his presence. So Ehud came to him. Now he was sitting alone in his cool roof chamber and Ehud said to him: 'I have a word from God for you.' So he arose from his seat. Then Ehud reached with his left hand and took the sword from his right thigh and thrust it into his belly, and the hilt followed the blade, and the fat closed over the blade for he did not withdraw the sword from his belly, and the contents came out. Then Ehud left by the vestibule and closed and locked the doors to the roof chamber upon him.

Just as he was leaving the servants arrived and saw that the doors to the roof chamber were locked and they said, 'Surely he is relieving himself in the closet of the cool chamber.' So they waited till they were embarrassed, but still he did not open the doors to the roof chamber, so they took the key and opened – and behold, their master was lying on the ground, dead. Ehud escaped while they delayed, passed the sculptured stones, and escaped to Seirah.

It is probably the most vulgar story in the Hebrew Bible and obviously not everyone's idea of a good laugh. There are wisdom motifs underlying it – the trick of the left-handed swordsman who manages to conceal his weapon, and then escape by making the guards assume that the king is still on the toilet! But the vulgarity starts with the overweight king himself who holds secret consultations on the toilet. That he is so fat that the sword completely disappears into his belly is the final touch, and a curious fate for Ehud's special double-edged sword. (Even the king's name may be significant, for an *egel* is a calf, some of which were specially nurtured and fattened as a delicacy.)

Perhaps the origins of this little story belong to the folk memory, and were passed on from generation to generation around a campfire, with the hearers laughing aloud as the sword disappeared. It is akin to the cartoon characters who explode or crush or otherwise destroy each other, only to scrape themselves together to reappear intact for the next scene, while the wily rabbit or mouse prepares to humiliate them again. The story is encased in its solemn framework: under Ehud's leadership Israel then attacked and defeated the Moabites and the land had rest for eighty years till Israel sinned again. But the humour remains in all its shameless vulgarity.

But the belly-laugh is not the norm. Nor is the witty one-liner, though there are a few of those as well. David is escaping from King Saul and takes refuge with the Philistines. While King Achish might have accepted him, his officers rightly point out that this David has fought against them in the past. David overhears and pretends to be mad, banging on the doors of the palace and dribbling into his beard (I Sam. 21.10–15). Achish is rightly annoyed and turns on his servants: 'Look, every time you see a crazy man, do you have to bring him to me?! I don't have enough of my own crazy people that you have to bring me this one to go crazy around me? Will you let this one into my house?' The sentence: 'I don't have enough of my own crazy people..?' needs a Woody Allen to deliver it. It is even more pointed when you realize that the word for 'crazy' is *meshuggeh*, a genuine Hebrew word that, via yiddish, has entered our own usage.

Sometimes the humour is sly. There are a whole series of stories where the hero encounters an angel of the Eternal, but is not utterly convinced that it really is an angel. The most blatant example is the story of the mother of Samson, a barren woman, who meets an angel who tells her that she will become pregnant. When she announces the news to her husband he is sufficiently skeptical to want to meet this 'angel' who has 'announced' her pregnancy. When the angel does appear, it requires him to disappear in a flash of fire before the husband is convinced. The story is recounted in Judges 13 and I have examined it in detail elsewhere.[3] But there are similar comical undertones to other such meetings with angels or divine manifestations, not least Moses' experience at the burning bush (Ex. 3). In all these cases the humour lies in the gap between what we, the readers, know is going on and the ignorance of the hero, half convinced but half sceptical about the encounter. The humour emerges most particularly in the case of Gideon, another 'judge/ saviour' who is summoned by an angel to defeat the Midianites. This angel also has to disappear in a flash of fire before Gideon is convinced. Gideon starts off on his military career, but is still rather frightened, and when confronting the Midianite army asks God for another sign. Look out for the catch in the following passage from Judg. 6.36–40:

> Then Gideon said to God: 'If You will deliver Israel by my hand as You have said, see, I am laying a fleece of wool on the threshing-floor, if there will be dew on the fleece alone, but the ground around it be dry, then I shall know that You will deliver Israel by my hand as You have said!' And it was so! When he got up early the following morning and squeezed the fleece, he wrung out dew from the fleece to fill a bowl with water.

At which point it must have struck Gideon that this was no great miracle – after all, a fleece will retain the dew long after the ground around it has dried up. So Gideon, understandably nervous, has another try.

> Then Gideon said to God: 'Do not let Your anger burn against me if I speak once again. Let me make a trial just this once with the fleece. Please let it be dry on the fleece alone, but let there be dew on the ground.' And God did so that night and it was dry on the fleece alone and upon the whole earth there was dew.

Notice that in the first version the text simply says: 'And it was so!', as indeed it should be. Now the Hebrew has 'And God did so' to point up that some action was required to reverse the natural order. Despite his inability to get it right the first time (or perhaps because of it since God constantly uses imperfect vessels in the Bible so as to prove that ultimately human success depends on divine intervention and power), Gideon goes on to victory.

All the above instances, except the case of Eglon, belong to a rather gentle kind of humour, a kind of sly folk wit at the expense of its heroes. But the Bible knows a different kind of rhetoric, often associated with the writings of the prophets, where a sharper, more satirical vein appears.

One of my favourite examples comes with the Isaiah of Jerusalem, someone who seems to have known at first hand the court circles that he mocks. Here he is describing the catastrophe that will happen when those who would normally want to take on a leadership role through the customary nepotism want nothing to do with it.

A man will grab hold of his brother in the house of his father: 'You have a robe, you be leader and this ruin can be in your hand!' [To appreciate the wit you have to know that the word translated here as 'ruin', *machshelah*, is a word play on the word for 'reign', *memshalah*, and that this whole sentence is a parody on the language used when high office was transferred – compare with Isa. 21.22.] But he will speak up on that day saying: 'I won't be the healer and in my house there is no bread and no robe. Don't make me the leader of the people!' (Isa. 3.6–7)

This same reversal of expectations underlies his condemnation of land speculators of his day.

Woe to those who join house to house, who add field to field until there is no room and you are made to live alone in the middle of the land. In my ear the Eternal one of hosts [has said]: 'Surely those many houses – will be desolate; great and fine ones – but with no-one living in them! (Isa. 5.8–9)

Measure for measure, those who buy up the land so as to have vast estates will indeed create large houses and tracts of land – but they will become totally empty.

He is particularly savage at the expense of the priests and prophets to whose ranks he belonged.

Woe up those who rise up early in the morning [ostensibly to pray] – but strong drink pursues them; who stay up late at night [for prayers] but wine inflames them. And they have lyre and harp, drum and flute and wine at their feasts – but the deed of the Eternal they do not observe, and the work of God's hand they do not see. [Though not named here as priests and prophets, the instruments listed here were used by the prophets to gain their visions – see I Sam. 10.5, and the priests had early morning and late night duties in the Temple. It is not simply that the former did not notice what God was doing, one of their titles was to be a 'seer', recognizing the hand of God in events was their actual task. And because they failed . . .] Therefore my people go into exile for want of knowledge. . . . [or else the latter phrase can mean, 'unconscious' since they, like their leaders, are too drunk to know!] (Isa. 5.11–13).

Isaiah goes on to attack others of the leadership:

Those who call bad good and good bad, darkness light and light dark, bitter sweet and sweet bitter.

Those who are wise – in their own eyes! and in their own sight – shrewd!

Those who are warriors (the military) – at drinking wine! and men of valour – at mixing strong drink!

Those who acquit the guilty – for a bribe; and deprive the innocent of their rights! (Isa. 5.20–23).

With Isaiah one feels the humour of an educated class, perhaps the world of the royal court where sharp wit and sophisticated wordplay might have their place. Jeremiah, a prophet but also a member of a priestly family, has a different literary style, but can be equally harsh in his views while similarly playing with the language of the covenant. The Jubilee year, as introduced in Leviticus 25, is to be a time when all debts are cancelled, all slaves are set free and all are to return to their original family lands.

You shall sanctify the fiftieth year and proclaim liberty (Hebrew *dror*) in the land for all its inhabitants, it shall be a Jubilee to you, and each of you shall return to his property and each shall return to his family (Lev. 25.10).

Now there is some doubt as to whether such a year of release ever took place historically, and indeed Jeremiah says as much on a particular occasion. The Babylonians are besieging Jerusalem and Jeremiah tells the king that the reason lies in their failure to carry out this law of releasing slaves and cancelling debts. He calls for an act of release and repentance.

The word which came to Jeremiah from the Eternal, after King Zedekiah had made a covenant with all the people in Jerusalem to make a proclamation of liberty (*dror*) to them, that everyone should set free his Hebrew slaves, male and female, so that no one should enslave a Jew, his brother. And they obeyed, all the princes and all the people who had entered into the covenant that everyone would set free his slaves, male or female, so that they would not be enslaved again; they obeyed and set them free. But afterwards [when the danger was past] they turned around and took back the male and female slaves they had set free and brought them into subjection as slaves (Jer. 34.8–11).

Then comes God's word to Jeremiah referring to the tradition of the sabbatical year when slaves would be released.

> You recently repented and did what was right in My eyes by proclaiming liberty (*dror*), each to his neighbour, and you made a covenant before Me in the house which is called by My name. But then you turned around and profaned My name when each of you took back his male and female slaves, whom you had set free according to their desire, and you brought them into subjection to be your slaves. Therefore, thus says the Eternal, you did not obey Me by proclaiming liberty (*dror*), each one to his brother and to his neighbour; so I will proclaim liberty (*dror*), an oracle of the Eternal, to the sword, to plague and to famine, and I will make you a horror to all the kingdoms of the earth (Jer. 34.15–17).

Jeremiah's phrasing is to pause with the word 'liberty', and then insert the standard prophetic formula, 'an oracle of the Eternal', before hitting his audience with the things that are indeed to be set free – the sword, plague and famine. It is magnificent rhetoric, invoking as it does the language of tradition subverted for his purpose. It is wit, but it is not funny.

Perhaps the commonest form of humour, however, is the irony to be found in the narrative materials of the Bible.[4] The irony lies again in the distance between our human perception of what we are doing and the 'reality' as seen from the divine perspective. Given this distance some traditions choose to moralize, but the Hebrew Bible rarely does this. Rather it sets side by side the two faces of reality and leaves it to the reader to recognize what is going on.

The builders of the tower of Babel believe that they are building a tower that will reach up to the very heavens (Gen. 11.4) – but God has to 'come down' (v. 5) in order to see this little city and its tower.

The classic example of sustained irony is the Book of Jonah which I have treated on a number of occasions.[5] Apart from the many details there are a number of overriding ironies in the story. Jonah, who runs away from Nineveh to avoid calling the wicked Ninevites to repentance, takes passage on a boat. God sends a supernatural storm, the sailors discover that Jonah is the cause and reluctantly throw him overboard, only to become God-fearers when the storm ceases. Jonah, in his flight to avoid God's will, has inadvertently converted a whole bunch of foreigners to his God. Saved by a fish, he finally, after three days, recites a psalm – which manages to do everything except acknowledge that he has run away from God in the first place. And he is indeed rescued from the fish – when it throws up at this exercise in pseudo-piety. Most dramatically, when Jonah finally gets to explain why he ran away in the first place, he spits into God's face the most powerful traditional statement about God's love, compassion and endless patience – a patience that has been more sorely tested by Jonah than by any of the pagans he has encountered. We will see how Jonah has an impact on later Jewish tradition in chapter 5.

Some modern critics have radically misunderstood the Book of Jonah, using the figure of the prophet as a stick with which to beat the Jewish people – as hating other nations. But who wrote the story if not a member of that people, deeply conscious of the risks of a narrow particularism? The universalism of the author parodies the particularism of his hero. The principle of self-criticism, that is the key to so much of the Hebrew Bible, is never more clearly expressed.

In the chapters that follow some aspects of this inner self-criticism are explored, through the biblical materials themselves and some Rabbinic views on them. Where better to begin than with the 'founding father' of Israel, Abraham himself, in all his complexity and self-contradiction.

2

Abraham and Justice

It is hard to know how to approach Abraham today. He is the quintessential patriarch, with all the positive and negative implications of that title. He is never young. Rather, he appears before us fully developed in his authority and power – the father of the Jewish people, the fighter for justice, the pioneer of faith, the beloved of God.

Curiously, when it comes to depicting Abraham in art, there are no images that come to mind where he stands by himself. There are celebrated classical portraits of Moses and David, but Abraham is always portrayed in the middle of some story: binding his son Isaac or sending away Hagar or meeting with the three heavenly messengers who will announce the birth of his long awaited child. But we do not see the man.

Yet if we examine the Abraham of the Hebrew Bible, we begin to see something of his complexity, at least in terms of the way that the biblical tradition has been handed down to us.

This is not the place to argue about the history of the traditions that make up the biblical account. The individual chapters or sections may have different provenance or sources; they may have a long pre-history, oral as well as literary, before they reached their final form; they may describe not one or indeed any real historical character, and may even be composites of many 'heroes' of early Israel; yet the final text that we have in Genesis 12–22 is organized to give a coherent and relatively consistent picture of the figure Israel identified as the father of the nation and the founder of the faith.

What is most striking today, and in many ways the most exciting feature of the description, is the variety of facets of his character that are displayed, even if so many are mutually contradictory. The reader has to decide if these represent a collection of fragments or the subversive hand of a single author. Yes, Abraham is a heroic figure, but he is by no means depicted as flawless. He has faith in God, but on a number of occasions acts in very human ways, even against the express word of God. Thus no sooner has he entered the land promised to him by God (Gen. 12) than he leaves it when famine strikes. God has promised him an offspring, yet he tries to guarantee it by taking Hagar as his second wife and having a child by her.

If these are evidence of inner contradictions in his character, there are occasions when his actions are of questionable morality. On two occasions he pretends that his wife is his sister, and the first time gains considerable financial benefit when the King of Egypt takes her. As always the text is open to interpretation, but here it seems pretty explicit. Abraham points out to his wife that because of her exceptional beauty the Egyptians might kill him and take her. So he begs her to claim that she is his sister '*that it may go well with me for your sake* and my soul go on living because of you' (Gen. 12.13). When Pharaoh does indeed take Sarah into his harem Abraham is well rewarded, and the Bible uses the exact phrase again '*and for Abraham it went well for her sake*' (Gen. 12.16), then goes on to list the sheep, cattle, male and female slaves, asses and camels that he acquires as a result (Gen. 12.16).

Perhaps even more shocking is the contradictory nature of his sense of justice. Seemingly at great personal risk he argues and pleads with God to spare the cities of Sodom and Gomorrah, doomed to destruction for the corruption and violence within them, if even ten honest men are to be found within them. And yet he is willing to suppress all questions of justice, or even human love, when it comes to offering his son Isaac as a sacrifice to God.

These tales represent no simple hero or ancestor worship. They propound riddles that have been addressed by every generation seeking to understand their relationship to Abraham.

The champion of justice and mercy

The inner contradictions that challenge the readers of these texts are particularly well illustrated by the issue of justice. The purpose for which God chose Abraham is spelled out in terms of the search for justice within the world. God debates whether to inform Abraham about the proposed destruction of Sodom and Gomorrah.

The Eternal said, Shall I conceal from Abraham what I am about to do? For Abraham will become a nation, great and powerful, and all the nations of the earth will be blessed through him; for I have known/chosen him so that he shall command his children and household after him that they keep the way of the Eternal, to do righteousness and justice (*tzedaqah umishpat*), so that the Eternal may bring to Abraham what He has promised him (Gen. 18.17–19).

The purpose of the choosing of Abraham, of promising him a great progeny and a land of his own, is to help establish the principles of righteousness and justice as the dominant force in the conduct of the nations of the world. Yet how do you set about creating such a value system? In what follows God tells Abraham that he is about to destroy Sodom and Gomorrah because of the wickedness that is within them. Abraham is called on to challenge God on two levels, both of equal importance for his education into his new role. Firstly to raise the issue of justice in such a case:

Then Abraham drew near and said, 'Will You really wipe out the good with the bad? Perhaps there are fifty good people within the city, will You wipe it out and not spare the place for the sake of the fifty good who are in it? Far be it from You to act like that! to kill good and bad together, treating good and bad alike. Far be it from You! Shall the Judge of all the earth not act justly!? (23.25).

We can feel as Abraham argues his mounting horror at the thought that God could act unjustly. The author puts into his mouth age old questions about the suffering of human beings and the quest to find some meaning in it. Surely God must be the source of it and must in some way be able to offer an explanation – but only if God's integrity can be trusted. And surely God's values cannot be less than human ones! In the discussion that follows, Abraham argues God down from fifty righteous people, a substantial number, to ten, the smallest unit that could be considered as a real group with power to influence a society. In the course of this negotiation Abraham is himself exploring the implications of what justice should mean and how a society is itself to be understood.

But alongside this exploration we see another struggle, as Abraham sets about challenging the justice of God. It is perhaps hard for us to understand the radical nature of this argument. In a culture where gods are the supreme powers and human beings are totally subordinate, Abraham's radical challenge to God's justice is an astonishing reversal of roles. Erich Fromm has expressed the implications of this:

> With Abraham's challenge a new element has entered the biblical and later Jewish tradition. Precisely because God is bound by the norms of justice and love, man is no longer his slave. Man can challenge God – as God can challenge man – because above both are principles and norms ... Abraham challenges God ... by accusing him of violating his own promises and principles. Abraham is not a rebellious Prometheus; he is a free man who has the right to demand, and God has no right to refuse.[1]

Fromm locates this freedom of Abraham in the covenant that exists between Abraham and God, a covenant that dignifies human beings with freedom. In this sense Abraham has accepted the freedom and responsibility given to Adam and Eve when they were cast out of the Garden of Eden. Human beings now carry total responsibility for their actions, they are accountable, but that gives them the right to demand the same accountability of God. It is this moment of standing up to God and arguing and asserting his position that is the second lesson of justice that Abraham is learning, and which he is to convey to those who come after him – the need to fight for justice against whatever powers stand in its way, up to and including God.

This subversive idea is recognized and made explicit in a Rabbinic comment on the phrase that has spelled out Abraham's challenge: 'Shall the Judge of all the earth not act justly?' It is glossed in the midrashic collection Genesis Rabbah (49.9):

> Just because there is no one who can prevent You, will You not do justice?

Here the limitations of human power over God are acknowledged, but also the lesson, that works on a human level as well, that justice should not merely be subsumed to power. God stands as guarantor of justice and human freedom over against all human powers, ideologies or systems that would demand exclusive authority, even when they claim to speak in the name of God.

There are innumerable Rabbinic statements about the qualities of Abraham that reflect his concern with justice in the world. He lived in the neighbourhood of Sodom because, knowing the way they mistreated the poor, he would look after those who suffered at their hands.[2] When God threatens to destroy Sodom, Abraham reminds God that after the flood he had promised never to bring a flood upon the earth. In line with a number of other midrashim the suggestion is made that God's promise only applied to a flood of water, but God had said nothing about a flood of fire! But Abraham argues that God cannot play with words in this way, a promise not to bring a flood to destroy the world is a promise, and God must adhere to it. Such was the sense of justice of Abraham, according to another midrash, that even his camels would not enter into a place where idolatry was practised! (*Avot D'Rabbi Natan* 8.8).

Yet the Abraham who pleads for justice, is also the one who pleads for mercy at the same time. In fact in biblical thought 'justice' and 'mercy' are complementary parts of a greater whole. The term *tzedeq*, righteousness and justice, is based on a strict sense of what is right and wrong, a distinction that must be exact and precise. It is best understood from the verse in Leviticus that demands 'Just scales, just weights, just measures, dry and wet' (Lev. 19.36). *umoznei tzedek avnei tzedek eifat tzedek v'hin tzedek*. It is the reliability of weights and measures that ensures the integrity of the entire system of human interaction, from the world of commerce to the highest levels of scientific measurement – and that integrity is at the heart of the term *tzedek*.

However the other term, *mishpat*, which is to be passed on by Abraham to his successors, has a broader range of meanings. It is used in a strictly legal context in a number of ways: it is the term for a court case, for the judgment that comes from it, for the sentence that is passed and the concept of justice itself. However part of its broader meaning is custom, the normative working of a system and the harmonious interaction of its parts. Thus a true judgment, *mishpat*, will be very precise about the particular crime that is being examined and will seek to discover the rights and wrongs, *tzedeq*. But having come to a correct conclusion, the broader idea of *mishpat* will then take into account the circumstances that led to the crime in the first place, the human and social background. Thus Isaiah will call upon the people to ensure that justice, *mishpat*, is done *on behalf of* the widow and orphan (Isa. 1.17). Precisely because they are without power in that society, more must be done to ensure their welfare and that they are not exploited. Thus mercy becomes the complement to strict judgments, in the broader concept of *mishpat*, justice.

This is the background needed to understand one of the best known midrashim about Abraham. Again it is based on our verse, 'Shall the judge of all the earth not act justly?' Abraham continues by saying:

> If it is strict justice that You want, then there can be no world (because no human being could survive such an absolutely strict judgment). So if You want the world to exist, You cannot expect absolutely strict justice. Do You want to hold the rope from both ends? You want the world to endure and You want justice as well. Unless You relent a little, the world will not endure (*Pesikta De-Rab Kahana* 19.3).

Thus the champion of justice, who demands strict justice from God, is also the champion of human reality and weakness – an idea already present in Abraham's defence of Sodom and Gomorrah, but spelled out here in this Rabbinic idea. Without compassion and mercy to temper strict justice, no human society could endure. Justice tempered with mercy is the Rabbinic view of the values brought into the world by Abraham.

The binding of Isaac

Yet this view of Abraham comes into direct conflict with the event that above all else stands out in his life, his willingness to sacrifice his son Isaac to God (Gen. 22). Since the story has so many echoes it is impossible to deal with it here in any detail. Even attempting to understand what the Bible intends with this story is difficult. Taken in isolation it is a shocking tale. God tells Abraham to take his only, beloved son and offer him up as a burnt offering on a distant mountain. Without any evidence of hesitation, Abraham prepares the wood, saddles his ass, takes two young men to accompany him and sets off with Isaac on a three day journey. When they arrive at the place, father and son head off to the place of the sacrifice: 'they went on, the two of them together'. Isaac asks his father, 'Here is the fire and the wood, but where is the lamb for the sacrifice?' In Abraham's ambiguous answer, 'God will provide the lamb (liter-

ally, 'will see for himself the lamb') for the sacrifice, my son', the
reader has to seek clues as to his emotional state. It may be that
Isaac also becomes fully aware of what is going on at this point. The
text simply repeats the poignant phrase, 'they went on, the two of
them together'. Seemingly without protest the son allows himself to
be bound upon the altar. It is only as Abraham's knife is about to
descend that an angel calls from heaven and stops him.

On one level the story as a whole appears to be a protest against
child sacrifice – Israel's God does not demand it. This would place it
in our category of 'extrinsic subversion', a biblical attack on the
religious conventions of its time. It has even been argued that
Abraham's willingness to kill his son is a reflection of his own
acceptance of that practice. A father had the power of life and death
over his child. How best show loyalty to a god than by sacrificing
one's own child? It takes this radical experience, up to the brink of
committing murder, to convince Abraham that this was not what his
God desired. The Rabbis assume that towards the climax Abraham
was so committed to the act that the angel had to call his name twice
to get his attention (Gen. 22.11)! Moreover they noted that the
angel says, 'Do not stretch out your hand against the lad', but adds
as well, 'nor do any harm to him.' Abraham was in such a fanatic
state at this moment, or so mad, that he asked, 'if I may not kill him,
can I at least draw blood to show my loyalty to God?'! 'Nor do any
harm to him!' came the reply.

However the story has also to be read within the cycle of
Abraham stories. The Rabbinic view is that the story comes as the
last of a whole series of tests in Abraham's life. From a more literary
point of view it can likewise be seen as the climax to a pattern
established by the sequence of narratives about him in the Book of
Genesis. Though Abraham is promised offspring, Sarah his wife is
barren, and at her suggestion, he takes Hagar, her Egyptian maid,
and hence the child Ishmael is born. Then Sarah herself conceives
and gives birth to Isaac. Ishmael is sent away, and all seems set for
the promise of God to be fulfilled, that Abraham will have a child
through Sarah to succeed him. Despite their attempt to 'guarantee'
the promise through their own actions and the birth of the 'wrong'
son Ishmael, who has to be sent away, God has brought about the
desired result. At this point, the 'happy end', God 'tests' Abraham,
as the text explicitly tells us (Gen. 22.1).[3]

What is this test? On one level it would appear to be a test of his trust in God now that all these events have taken place. Even if God now asks that Abraham sacrifice Isaac, to take away the son upon whom the entire promise depends, is he prepared to trust that God's promise will nevertheless be fulfilled? Abraham comes through the test, and by his willingness to give up his son to God, actually wins him for the future.

The biblical account seems to have no doubts about the probity of Abraham's actions, though it is possible to recognize a degree of ambiguity under the surface. It is present, for example, in the changing names of God in the story. Here we have to enter into a brief note about the use of the divine names in the Hebrew Bible. There are two names that occur most frequently. One is *elohim* which serves as a general term for 'the gods' and other 'powers', but also for the 'One God' of the universe. It is the word most commonly translated as 'God'. The other term, made up of four Hebrew letters (*yod-he-vav-he*) is known therefore as the 'tetra-grammaton' and in modern translations is simply transliterated as YHWH or written as 'Yahweh'. This name is the Israelite term for that same 'One God' of the Universe, *elohim*, but in the identity that they recognized as uniquely related to themselves. An early tradition forbade the uttering of that name aloud except by the High Priest and so it was substituted with the word *adonai* which means 'Lord', and hence the conventional word used for God in many translations. (I prefer to use a convention that sees in this name a form of the Hebrew verb *hayah*, to be, and hence the translation 'the Eternal'.) But why is one or other of these two names used in a particular context – and why do they sometimes interchange within a given passage?

Bible scholars of the historical-critical school of the past few centuries postulated that these two different names reflected two or more different ancient traditions about the name of God that were inherited by the compilers of the Bible who edited them together. So this chapter of Genesis, with its two versions of the name, would reflect such a 'compound' text. However, apart from major problems with the theory itself, it offers no satisfactory explanation as to the use of the different names of God in this particular chapter. If we accept that some kind of meaning lies behind the usage, what is significant here is that it is as *elohim* that God 'tests' Abraham – a usage that is consistent throughout the first part of the story. But it is an angel of YHWH that stops him. In fact there is a specific play on this changing name in that Abraham explains to Isaac that *elohim* (God) will 'see to', will provide, the lamb for the sacrifice, *elohim yir'eh* (22.8); but in the end Abraham calls the place YHWH *yir'eh* (22.14), 'the Eternal will see'.

Elsewhere in the Pentateuch a similar distinction is made between the two names of God in connection with another set of contradictory messages coming from God. The prophet Balaam is invited to 'curse' Israel, and though he wants to 'God', *elohim*, forbids him (Num. 22.12). When a second lot of messengers invite him *elohim* gives permission, but then *elohim* gets angry when he goes and an angel of YHWH stops him, almost killing Balaam in the process. In the end Balaam is forced to bless Israel instead of cursing them (Num. 22–24). Here, too, the switching between the names seems to reflect the contradictory inner wishes of Balaam and the express 'outer' wishes of God. That is to say, the use of the two names may be a way of expressing different psychological or spiritual states within a particular character.

If we accept this view for the time being, we could suggest that the *elohim* who 'commands' Abraham to sacrifice his son is actually a wish that comes from within him, as if he feels the need to show his loyalty and faithfulness through this act. It is 'the angel of the Eternal', YHWH, who has to stop him.

This approach to the different use of the divine names is actually a modern variant on the Rabbinic view that the two names represent two different aspects of God, along the lines of the two attributes we noted above. Within God is the attribute of strict justice, which can be seen, they taught, whenever the name *elohim* is used. But God also contains the attribute of mercy, and this is to be found wherever the name YHWH appears in the text. On this reading it is indeed God as strict judge who imposes this trial upon Abraham in the first part of the story, but God's mercy intervenes to stop him performing the final act.

Clearly the Rabbis were no less perturbed by this story than a modern reader and they wrote many comments trying to explain it. They focussed on Abraham's three-day journey to the place of sacrifice, a time period that is simply passed over by the biblical text. Their stories ask, what was Abraham thinking during that time? How did his natural sense of justice react to it? Did he protest? Was he tempted to give up his God in the light of this impossible task? They even noticed that Isaac is not mentioned at all at the end of the chapter when Abraham goes home, and asked whether Abraham actually killed him, Isaac being resurrected afterwards.

With the Rabbinic treatment of this and other problematic episodes in the lives of the patriarchs we can see a tendency towards apologetics, the justification of the 'apparent' wrongdoings of the founding generations. Sometimes this is out of a deep respect for their memory, sometimes because the Rabbis are locked in a major religious struggle with those who would denigrate them and their traditions. The subversive honesty of the biblical text is robbed of its power to shock and disturb. What fascinates about the Rabbinic approach to commentary, however, is their realization of the danger of either explaining away a problem in the text or restricting the ways in which it could be understood. Their respect for its integrity, it being for them, after all, the direct word of God, led them to the observation that 'the text never loses its original meaning' or 'the meaning it has within its original context' (Shabbat 63a). However many layers of interpretation are spread over it, the original text is always there to be rediscovered.

Nevertheless there is clearly a danger in this story in so far as Abraham is a model for the generations that follow and such zeal and potential fanaticism could prove highly dangerous. So the Rabbis were very careful to insist that whereas other qualities of Abraham should be imitated, his hospitality to strangers, his missionary activity, this was a once-and-for-all event. No one else should imagine that they were called upon to sacrifice their child to God. The merit Abraham acquired for his obedience to God was available to help the Jewish people from then on.

However Jewish history moves on and new situations require new interpretations. In the Middle Ages when Jewish communities in the Rhineland were destroyed by the crusaders, people turned to the *Akedah*, the 'binding of Isaac' as it came to be known (not the 'sacrifice' of Isaac!) and compared themselves to Abraham – only they felt that they had sacrificed even more than he had because their children had indeed been killed. Poetry created for the Synagogue liturgy at this time is full of this thought. It is explored in *The Last Trial* by Shalom Spiegel, a brilliant study of the theme of the *Akedah* in midrash and liturgy. He quotes from these liturgical poems:

Before that patriarch could in his haste sacrifice his only one,

It was heard from heaven: Do not put forth your hand to destroy!
But now how many sons and daughters of Judah are slain –
While yet He makes no haste to save those butchered nor those
cast on the flames.
(*R. Eliezer bar Joel ha-Levi*)

On the merit of the *Akedah* at Moriah once we could lean,
Safeguarded for the salvation of age after age –
Now one *Akedah* follows another, they cannot be counted.
(*R. David bar Meshullam*)[4]

It is as if the strangeness and indeed shock of this story evokes
attempts in every generation to relate to it anew. If we jump to the
twentieth century the psychiatrist Erich Wellisch suggests that the
'*Akedah* motif' is a solution to the Oedipus complex described by
Freud. Whereas Freud focussed on what he saw as the rivalry and
subsequent hatred that the son has for his father in early childhood,
Wellisch points to the practice of infanticide by fathers because of
their fear of being overthrown, ousted from power and leadership.
Infanticide, in this reading, was a prevention against patricide, but
was often rationalized by the belief that the gods demanded it and
were pleased by it. Conscious or unconscious wishes about infanticide persisted in ancient times and even until today, but Abraham
solves them with the episode of the *Akedah*. 'Until Abraham the
father's authority was based on fear. Since Abraham it has been
based on love. After the *Akedah*, Abraham realizes that God
demands life not death.'[5]

Another psychological view is given by Rabbi David Polish who
links the story, as indeed does the Bible, to the sending away of
Ishmael in the previous chapter. It is Abraham's overwhelming
sense of guilt at this previous act that makes him take on this self-
punishing act of sacrificing Isaac. Conversely a theologian like Ignaz
Maybaum recognizes in Abraham a basic trust in the integrity,
reliability, justice and goodness of God. Despite the command he
knows that in the end God will save the child. Indeed the biblical
text can also be cited to justify this view when Abraham tells the
young men that he and Isaac will go to make the sacrifice and 'we'
will come back to you (22.5).

Perhaps one final reading will be helpful to show how the story
can be transformed. The Israeli poet Amir Gilboa has written a
poem called 'Isaac' that takes some of the biblical imagery and even

words and retains its subversive power by radically reversing the content of the story:

> At dawn, the sun strolled in the forest
> together with me and father
> and my right hand was in his left.

> Like lightning a knife flashed among the trees.
> And I am so afraid of my eyes' terror, faced by blood on the leaves.
> Father, father, quickly save Isaac
> so that no one will be missing at the midday meal.

> It is I who am being slaughtered, my son,
> and already my blood is on the leaves.
> And father's voice was smothered and his face was pale.

> And I wanted to scream, writhing not to believe,
> and tearing open my eyes.
> And I woke up.

> And my right hand was drained of blood.[6]

In this poem it is not Isaac who is sacrificed but Abraham himself. The father in the poem is both the patriarch and the poet's own father who was murdered during the Holocaust.

There is no satisfactory conclusion to the discussion of this remarkable biblical chapter. Indeed the fact that it is a key reading for the Jewish New Year Festival ensures that the riddles and difficulties it contains are propounded and publicly discussed year after year – but it is also part of the daily readings in the Jewish morning service. Thus religious Jews are faced with rediscovering, challenging or acknowledging Abraham year in and year out, and in this very particular sense he is alive to every Jewish generation as almost no other biblical character.

Abraham and Ishmael

If the story of the 'binding of Isaac' is problematic when examining Abraham's commitment to justice, just as problematic is his and Sarah's treatment of his firstborn son Ishmael. From the biblical narrative it is evident that Ishmael is a 'mistake' that should never have happened if Abraham had simply been a bit more patient and waited for Sarah to have a child. But part of the power of the Hebrew Bible is precisely in its readiness to face the realities of human actions. Abraham sends Hagar and Ishmael away and, whether or not he gives them ample provisions, Hagar loses her way in the desert and the child almost dies. An angel also rescues Ishmael, in a direct parallel to the story of the angel who saved Isaac from being sacrificed, and he too is promised a great future. Indeed since he is also the son of Abraham following the promise that many nations would arise from him, it is no surprise to learn later in the Bible that Ishmael becomes the father of twelve nations (Gen. 25.16). Ishmael is to be blessed in exactly the same way as Abraham's other descendant Jacob who bears twelve sons that will become the twelve tribes. In this respect at least there is a symmetry between the two lines of Abraham's descendants. According to the Hebrew Bible Isaac and Ishmael met again at least once when they came together to bury Abraham (Gen. 25.9).

The Rabbis had difficulties with the story of Ishmael as well and felt the need to justify Abraham and Sarah's behaviour. Thus they read into Ishmael's 'playing' with the young Isaac (Gen. 21.9) a range of unacceptable behaviour. Some of the Rabbinic attitudes must have a historic context in the struggles of the Jewish people with their neighbours. At a later period Ishmael becomes paradigmatic of the Arab world just as Esau, Jacob's twin brother, comes to stand for Rome. But it is in this century that Abraham's treatment of Ishmael comes again into focus as the Jewish people and the State of Israel seek to understand their relationship to the Arab world. This is a subject beyond the concerns of this book, but I would like to tell a personal story that illustrates how these seemingly irrelevant ancient stories can spring to life in unexpected ways and require a new response.

I spoke as part of a panel at one of the first Jewish–Christian–Muslim meetings in Berlin, some time at the end of the 1960s. In the question time a young man got up and said he was a Palestinian and wanted to ask me something. I assumed it would be a political question of some sort, but he said it was something quite different. He had read the Hebrew Bible and particularly the stories of Abraham, Isaac and Ishmael. His problem was that in these stories Ishmael, who was the ancestor of the Arab peoples, was the rejected son of Abraham's unwanted wife, Hagar – so how could he identify with the Jewish people?

The question was important in many ways. Jews are used to the historical sequence of Judaism, then Christianity and then Islam. In that sequence Jews may feel the need to confront Christians in particular, but sometimes also Muslims, with the way in which Jews are depicted in their holy scriptures. But we readily assume that since neither Christianity or Islam existed till long after the Hebrew Bible was written, there cannot be any equivalent problems of our depiction of them. Of course, from a historical point of view, that is absolutely true. But in so far as the Hebrew Bible contains the sustaining myth of the Jewish people and thus, in some sense, defines their attitude to others, the texts of the Hebrew Bible are indeed still alive. And whatever attitude, if any, Jews may have to them, others do see them as representative of Jewish belief and practice. What the Bible says about Ishmael, just as what it says about the boundaries of the Holy Land, has a reality again today that it has not had for centuries. So where are the contemporary Jewish commentaries on the Bible that address a Jewish way of understanding these texts and what do they say?

In this particular case I was able to answer the young Palestinian because my own experience of dialogue had at least introduced me to this kind of problem. Traditional scriptures cannot be removed but they can be transformed by the way they are interpreted. As I mentioned before, the story of the binding of Isaac, but also the preceding chapter on Hagar and Ishmael, are read during the Jewish New Year Festival, Rosh Hashanah. In collaboration with Rabbi Lionel Blue I co-edited the High Holyday prayerbook of the Reform Synagogues of Great Britain, and as part of the work produced a commentary to the biblical readings, using traditional and modern materials. Being aware of the problem of reconciliation between Israel and the Arab world, and the need for a symbolic enactment of this within the liturgy, I had included a poem by the Israeli poet Shin Shalom. He draws on the parallel fate of the two brothers, both threatened by death and rescued at the last moment by a divine emissary.

Ishmael, my brother,
How long shall we fight each other?

My brother from times bygone,
My brother – Hagar's son,
My brother, the wandering one.

One angel was sent to us both,
One angel watched over our growth –
There in the wilderness, death threatening through thirst,
I a sacrifice on the altar, Sarah's first.

Ishmael, my brother, hear my plea:
It was the angel who tied thee to me . . .

Time is running out, put hatred to sleep.
Shoulder to shoulder, let's water our sheep.[7]

Abraham and Melchizedek

One of the powerful things about the biblical narratives about
Abraham is that they convey with great simplicity both his private
life and his relationship with others in the society around him. He is
clearly a man of status and power having access to the rulers of the
local lands (Gen. 21.22). We see him making alliances with local
chieftains (Gen. 14.13) for mutual defence. He negotiates with the
local people to acquire a plot of land for a family burial place (Gen.
23.8–18). He acquires a well and is prepared to confront the local
chieftain when it is stolen by his servants (Gen. 21.25). Only once
does evidence of some deeper conflict surface in Abraham's
relations with the local Canaanites. Again it centres on the city of
Sodom and predates his debate with God about its destruction.
Following a local war (Gen. 14) Abraham appears in a quite
different guise as a military figure leading a coalition of his covenant
partners to rescue his nephew Lot. The successful Abraham returns
from his victory to encounter two figures: Melchizedek, king of
Salem, the future Jerusalem, and the unnamed King of Sodom.
With the latter, whether from personal animosity or moral judgment because of the activities of Sodom, Abraham wishes to have
no obligations.

> The king of Sodom said to Abraham, Give me the persons but
> keep the goods for yourself. But Abram said to the king of
> Sodom: I have raised my hand (sworn) to the Eternal El Elyon
> (God Most High), maker of heaven and earth that neither a
> thread nor a sandal-thong, nor anything that is yours will I take,
> lest you should say 'I made Abram rich!'. I will take nothing
> except that which the young men have eaten and the share due to

the men who went with me; let Aner, Eshkol and Mamre take their share (Gen. 14.21–24).

And yet when it is necessary, Abraham will stand before God and plead for the saving of Sodom even if only a few righteous people are to be found within it.

Conversely in Melchizedek Abraham finds a colleague who shares in some way his own religious convictions. It is also a somewhat guarded conversation in which Abraham recognizes in El Elyon, Melchizedek's 'Most High God', the God that Abraham himself has encountered (Gen. 14.18–20, 22).

Abraham's origins are only briefly mentioned and nothing at all is said about how he came to obey the voice that said to him, *lekh l'kha*, 'Go, for yourself, from your land!' How did Abraham come to be a believer and what was the background out of which he came? The Bible itself tells us that Abraham's father was an idol-worshipper (Josh. 24.2) and the Rabbis filled in this story in an attempt to explain Abraham's journey. They thought that he came to the conclusion that there was only one God from his own observations of the world. On seeing the sun he thought it was the mighty creator of the world, but at night it disappeared to be replaced by the moon and stars, so he thought the moon was the creator of everything. But the next day it too disappeared, so he understood that some greater power had created both. He reached his awareness of God through both reason and inspiration.

The most famous Rabbinic story about his youthful iconoclasm has its echoes in Islamic sources. Abraham's father Terah used to manufacture idols. One night Abraham smashed them up and left the hammer in the hand of the largest. When Terah asked what happened he explained that they had fought over the offerings made to them and the large idol had destroyed the others. Terah told him that this was utter nonsense as they were unable to do anything at all! 'Let my father's ears hear what his mouth says', said Abraham.

In these stories Abraham is the discoverer of monotheism, a revolutionary who brings a new idea into the world. But the Bible is again subversive in its willingness to admit that other figures, non-Israelites, can also have the same experience of God. It is notable that the two pivotal leaders Abraham and Moses both encounter such figures and have a positive relationship with them: Abraham and Melchizedek; Moses and Jethro his father-in-law. Such openness will have its positive consequence in Rabbinic thought. They taught that the righteous of all nations have a place in the world to come. Though there are also expressions that are antagonistic to Gentiles in Rabbinic literature, the main thrust of their views can be found in the debate about what was the greatest biblical verse. The great Rabbi Akiva thought it was the phrase, 'you shall love your neighbour as yourself' (Lev. 19.18); but his colleague, Ben Azzai, argued that even greater was the sentence in Gen. 5.1:

> These are the generations of Adam, of humanity; when God created the first human being God made him in the image of God.

All human beings are created in God's image so all are equal before God. Hence Rabbinic sayings like the following:

> The righteous among the gentiles are priests of God.

> I call heaven and earth to witness that whether it be gentile or Israelite, man or woman, slave or handmaid, according to the deeds they do, so will the Holy Spirit rest on them.[8]

Abraham remains a riddle in the complexity of his character captured by these accounts. We see him as the father of a specific people, but at the same time a model of universal humanity. We have seen him as the fighter for justice for the wicked city of Sodom, though he evidently views the place with distaste, prepared even to challenge God and demand that God adhere to the values that are to be introduced to humanity. Alongside that sense of justice is also a feeling of compassion that was to be developed in the Rabbinic view of him. Yet at the moment when we might domesticate Abraham, make him too nice and one-dimensional, we find his dark side, the singleminded fanaticism, also very human, that would allow him to sacrifice his son and only withdraw at the last moment.

There are other Abrahams we could have examined, for there is more to say about his domestic life, his relationship to the land that has been promised to him, and even more about his faith. But as I have suggested the biblical picture is many-faceted and each facet has had its echo in Rabbinic and later Jewish tradition. Perhaps the point I would like to make above all else is that he remains open for investigation, interpretation and challenge even today. The biblical account itself subverts any simple one-dimensional view of him that would put him out of our reach to question and criticize at the same time that we admire him.

When his name is changed by God from Avram to Avraham, the Bible tells us that this is a word play – for he will be *av hamon goyim*, 'the father of many nations'. Reflected in this title are the many manifestations of the Jewish people throughout the centuries, but also the 'nations' of Christianity and Islam that claim descent from him. If the title bestowed on Moses by the Jewish people is *Moshe Rabenu*, Moses our teacher, Abraham has also earned the title by which he is known in Jewish tradition, *Avraham avinu*, Abraham our father.

3

Exodus and Liberation

It is probably the most familiar story in the Hebrew Bible – the escape of the children of Israel from the clutches of the wicked Pharaoh of Egypt. As we discussed in our introductory chapter it has echoes way beyond its origins: in the songs of the slaves in the American South seeking their freedom; in the liberation movements of South America; in the struggle of Jews to leave the former Soviet Union under the motto, 'Let My people go!' Wherever the Bible has had its direct or indirect influence and wherever people have been enslaved to others, the story of the Exodus has come to give hope to the oppressed and to haunt their oppressors.

Many of the details have also entered the popular mind. The massacre of the male Israelites on Pharaoh's orders; the ten plagues, climaxing with the death of the firstborn, that broke the spirit of Pharaoh and his people; the crossing of the Sea of Reeds that opened before the Israelites but closed over the pursuing Egyptian chariots to drown them. And above all the vision of a promised land to which they were going, a land where slavery would never again exist, where all would be free.

If those are the elements that are remembered, there are any number of details that tend to be overlooked, and yet the essence of biblical texts lies precisely in their details. For here lie the qualities and values that underpin the broad sweep of the narrative and give it its subversive power. Even a superficial reading of the opening of the Exodus story highlights the fact that the heroines of the story are the women who took great personal risks and thereby changed the course of history. The midwives, Shifrah and Puah, refused to obey Pharaoh's genocidal orders and stood their ground when confronted by him (Ex. 1.15–22). Jochebed, the mother of Moses, hid the newborn child till it was no longer possible (Ex. 2.1–3). Miriam, his sister, watched over the child in its frail reed boat and dared to approach the daughter of Pharaoh (Ex. 2.4, 7). She, in turn, was willing to go against the express command of her father and adopt a Hebrew male child (Ex. 2.5–9). Before the story of the Exodus proper even begins we find a series of elements in the biblical narrative emphasizing the role of women that run totally counter to what might be expected given the patriarchal nature of biblical society. One may debate the primary reason for this. Is it that the biblical authors sought to honour these particular women, who were, incidentally, both Hebrews and Egyptians, and the role they played? Or is it part of another biblical convention of inverting all expectations about where power is to be discovered once God takes a hand in events – the secondborn son is frequently chosen over the firstborn who might be expected to inherit had God not willed otherwise; and here women, the weakest in society, overturn the plans of Pharaoh, the most powerful, who is doubly dishonoured by this.

Knowing the end result of the Exodus story we almost feel sorry for Pharaoh – he is, after all, only a mortal who thinks that he is a god competing with the real God, creator of the universe. But only Moses knew that at the outset of his challenge to the power of Egypt, and he had his doubts (Ex. 3.13–4.17). The Israelites were not convinced at all – and when things became worse after Moses' intervention they called on God to judge him:

> You have made us stink in the eyes of Pharaoh and his minions, you have put a sword in his hand to kill us! (Ex. 5.21).

But were they not already dying in their slave labour in the fields and their children being murdered by the regime? Pharaoh needed no further excuse to kill them. But slaves, by definition, cannot see beyond their slavery. The biblical perception of their psychology is painfully honest. In commenting on aspects of the Jewish Passover ritual, which recounts the story of the Exodus, Joseph B. Soloveitchik captures the essence of this state:

> A slave is a man without options. He cannot make his own decisions, except in insignificant areas. So his discernment in important matters is impaired. He never develops faith in his own judgment because it is never tested and sharpened practically. Trial-and-error experiences which build confidence and refine perception are absent. Only the free man is continually challen-

ged by the many possibilities in all aspects of life. Those who are
restricted in the scope of their choices or participation tend to
develop illusions; they see truth subjectively; they observe things
not as they are, but as they (the slaves) would like them to be . . .

A slave also lives in a constant state of fear because he is subject
to the mercurial will of his master. Thus, anxiety persists even if
there is no overt threat or actual attempt at intimidation. It is a
perpetual tension inherent in his status . . . He will therefore
intuitively prevent himself from ever contradicting his master, for
fear of provoking his anger. It becomes a reflex act of fear and
distrust.[1]

It took someone like Moses who had grown up as a free man in
the court of Pharaoh to lead the Israelites out to freedom.

Again the details of the story point up the underlying state of
mind. At every obstacle the Israelites wanted to turn back. In the
wilderness they became quite nostalgic for the 'good old days':

If only we'd died at the hand of the Eternal in the land of Egypt
when we sat by the flesh pots and ate our fill of bread (Ex. 16.3).

A careful reading of this verse indicates that though they *sat* by the
'flesh pots' (of the Egyptians) it was not the 'flesh' that they ate but
only bread! Present difficulties suppress the memory of past
troubles.

Though the narrative only hints at it, the Rabbinic tradition
points to a darker side of the Exodus itself. The Rabbis went as far
as to suggest that there were many who did not want to leave Egypt
at all. They had made a successful adjustment to life in Egypt and
did not wish to jeopardize their situation of relative power. A
disturbing Rabbinic legend explains that that was the reason for the
plague of three days of utter darkness. Under cover of the dark God
killed those who refused to leave so that their deaths would not be
seen by the Egyptians (Exodus Rabbah 14.3). The Exodus had to
appear to be unanimous. Every revolution has its victims.

But as well as the 'promised land' that was to be the goal of the
Israelites, and the new society they were to establish there, there is
another motivation for the events that run through the Exodus
story. That Egypt too shall come to know the liberating power of
God. If Egypt was the supreme world power of its time, then the
lesson of the Exodus was to be universal – all the world, all those

who oppress and all who are oppressed, are to see and take heed. Centuries later, when Israel was suffering another exile in Babylon and yearning to return to their land, another prophetic voice would recall this wider task.

> God said to me, it is too little a thing for you to be My servant, just to raise up the tribes of Jacob and to bring back the dispersed of Israel – for I have made you a light of the nations that My salvation may go out to the ends of the earth' (Isa. 49.6).

God's hand is not against the Egyptian people alone in the story of the Exodus, but also against their entire system of slavery as it is personified in their gods. Like the Pharaoh who 'did not know/ acknowledge Joseph' (Ex. 1.8) his successor mocked Moses at their first encounter:

> Who is 'the Eternal' that I should listen to His voice to let Israel go? I do not know/acknowledge the Eternal! (Ex. 5.2).

The Rabbis had him looking through a book listing all the 'gods' in the world and finding no mention of the name of the Eternal (Exodus Rabbah 5.14). It is a Rabbinic joke, but nevertheless a reminder that Pharaoh's Egypt had its social scientists, libraries and research institutes as befits an ancient imperial power. Moses replied that you do not find the living amongst the dead. His God could not be limited to the pages of a book. So Pharaoh had to learn the hard way to 'know/acknowledge' the Eternal, for his own sake but also to teach the rest of the world about a new kind of social system Israel was to pioneer on its land.

So the story could not end there. Each detail was lovingly preserved in the text of the Hebrew Bible and the biblical tradition itself insisted that the events be relived each year through a range of symbolic acts, and that the story be handed down to each successive generation.

> When your children say to you, 'What does this service mean to you?' you shall say, 'It is the Passover sacrifice to the Eternal who passed over the houses of the children of Israel in Egypt . . .' (Ex. 12.26–27).

> You shall tell your son on that day, it was because of this that the Eternal did for me when I came out of Egypt (Ex. 13.8).

When your son asks you tomorrow, saying, 'What is this?' you
shall say to him, 'With a strong hand the Eternal brought me out
of Egypt from the house of slavery' (Ex. 13.14).

So elaborate would the ritual of remembrance become that the
'son' of a later generation would ask a more technical question:

'What are the testimonies, the laws and judgments which the
Eternal your God commanded you?' (Deut. 6.20).

These four biblical verses, understood as four different questions
requiring answers, entered the Jewish Passover Haggadah, the
order of 'telling' that accompanies the family feast of remembrance,
the Seder evening. The questions will be identified with four types
of child, characters in the drama of the evening: the wise, the
wicked, the simple and the one too young even to ask. The biblical
hints will become realized in this family night that still retains its
power – when each of those present should consider themselves as if
they had personally come out of Egypt. Freedom was not lightly
won and is not kept without an active remembrance in each and
every generation.

But what are the participants in this ritual to remember on the
Passover night? They are to tell the story of the Exodus but the
Rabbis disagreed on where the story should begin, when did the
slavery start. They ruled that the ritual should begin the telling with
a situation that was shameful and end with one that was praise-
worthy. The end is clearly 'freedom', but what is there to be ashamed
about if one is enslaved by a greater power? Surely it was a matter
over which one had no control. If anyone had reason to be ashamed
about his actions it should be Pharaoh, the perpetrator, not the
victims! The Rabbis came up with two different understandings of
this 'shameful' beginning to the Exodus story, and as was their
custom, preserved both versions.

According to one, 'We were slaves to Pharaoh in Egypt but the
Eternal our God led us out from there with a strong hand and an
outstretched arm . . .' Thus the situation of physical slavery itself is
the shameful past that should be remembered and reflected upon
year after year in this ritual remembering. Unlike the celebration of
the heroic origins of a particular nation or people that is more often
the case, the Jewish people are to contemplate their physical
bondage and all the implications that follow from this situation.

The other introduction, however, goes back before the Exodus to the origins of Abraham and his family before him:

> In the beginning our ancestors were idol-worshippers, but now God has brought us near to God's service, as it is written: 'Joshua said to all the people, Thus says the Eternal God of Israel, In days of old your ancestors lived beyond the Euphrates, Terah the father of Abraham and the father of Nahor, and they served other gods (Josh. 24.2)'.

Once again the subversive challenge of the biblical narrative itself has had a direct impact on subsequent traditional understanding.

With these two different approaches to the 'beginnings' of the Exodus story, a central theme of the Passover becomes clear – that there are two kinds of slavery: the physical enslavement to a regime but also spiritual slavery, as expressed by the worship of idols. Both are deeply interlinked and both have to be addressed. The 'gods of Pharaoh' must also be defeated in this ever recurring struggle for liberation.

This double level of 'enslavement' seems to be addressed already in the Hebrew Bible in the two versions of the Ten Commandments, in Exodus and in Deuteronomy. There are some minor textual variations between them, sometimes in matters of letters or the order of words, but these are of little consquence. However there is one major difference when it comes to the reason given for the commandment to 'Observe' (Deut. 5.12) or 'Remember' (Ex. 20.8) the Sabbath day. The Exodus version is understood to be the 'religious' justification for setting aside the seventh day for rest:

> ... for in six days the Eternal made the heavens and the earth, the sea and everything that is in it and rested on the seventh day therefore the Eternal blessed the seventh day and made it holy (Ex. 20.11).

In contrast the Deuteronomy version stresses the socio-political reasons why this day of rest should be kept:

> Remember that you were a slave in the land of Egypt and the Eternal your God brought you out from there with a strong hand and an outstretched arm. Therefore the Eternal your God commanded you to make the Sabbath day' (Deut. 5.15).

From my teacher, Rav Sperber, in Jerusalem I learnt that the significance of both these views was to be echoed centuries later in the biblical account of the prophecies of Jeremiah about the imminent destruction of Jerusalem. For the prophet the Babylonian army was only an agent of God to bring about a punishment the people deserved for abusing and largely abandoning their covenant with God. No military alliances could protect them if the people were not able to change the inner life of their society. Two commandments represented the 'bottom line' that would make the difference between their survival or destruction, the Sabbath regulations and those concerning the release of slaves. So Jeremiah preached about the central importance of the preservation of the Shabbat, the day which dramatized the setting aside of labour as a sign of total submission to the will of God alone:

> Thus says the Eternal, guard your souls and do not carry burdens on the Sabbath day and bring them into the gates of Jerusalem. Bring no burden out of your houses on the Sabbath day and do no work and make the Sabbath day holy as I commanded your ancestors . . . then kings will come through the gates of this city and princes will sit on the throne of David . . . otherwise I will rain down fire on her gates and it will devour the palaces of Jerusalem and not cease (Jer. 17.21–27).

The other commandment that Jeremiah prioritized concerned the release of slaves in the seventh year – and we have seen in chapter 1 how savagely he attacked the leadership for betraying it.

God speaks there, through Jeremiah, with all the irony and savagery of wounded pride. The message is clear. Freedom is the essential constituent of the society that is to be established under the covenant with God. To betray that is to betray everything that was at the heart of the Exodus. But what is the guarantor of that freedom, the essential element that is to underpin it? Nothing less that the equality of all human beings as creations of God, and this creatureliness is symbolized by the Sabbath day. To keep the Sabbath is to acknowledge God as creator of the world and of all humanity. It is also to set aside human enslavement to nature, to the need to struggle daily to work and earn and survive. It is to assert that the purpose of human existence is more than that. To betray it is to betray the whole experiment that began with the Exodus.

The two themes, creation and Exodus, are deeply intertwined. The crossing through the Sea of Reeds to freedom, the breaking of the waters, is a powerful image of birth. But it is also an echo of the earlier moment of creation when God separated the upper and lower waters and gathered the lower ones together so that dry land may appear (Gen. 1.6, 9). This laconic description in Genesis, of God the artist/craftsman working with the raw materials that yield to the divine word, is in remarkable contrast to the creation legends of other Ancient Near Eastern cultures, as we have noted above. The very structure of the chapter with its repeated formulaic phrases expresses the same detached craftsmanship and control.

God said ... and it was so ... God saw that it was good ... it was evening and morning. . . .

The formalism conceals the extraordinary process of selection that has excluded so much mythological material in this description. Only elsewhere in the Bible, in poetic and prophetic writings, do we see hints of the cosmic battles of the creation myths of the Ancient Near East. For the waters that seemingly part so easily before the word or wind of God were elsewhere the raging powers of the storm gods that had to be tamed if order was to emerge out of primordial chaos.

Awake, awake, gird on strength, O arm of the Eternal!
Awake as in days of old, generations of the past!
Was it not You that split the monster, that pierced the dragon.
Was it not You that cleaved the sea, the waters of the great deep; who prepared in the depths of the sea a way for the redeemed to pass over?

(Isa. 51.9–10).

That Israel's God could stand apart from the created world, could control the forces of nature and express the divine will in the changes of history and in the rise and fall of earthly kingdoms, was a hard won understanding. Yet ultimately this divine engagement with the world and apartness reflects the paradox of our own human existence – eternally bound within our own creatureliness, sharing our physical nature with the animal world, yet somehow able to transcend it through the extraordinary power of our intellect and imagination. A number of Rabbis are credited in the midrash with the following expression of this tension:

God created human beings with four qualities of the higher beings [angels]: they stand upright, speak, understand and see. (But do not animals also see? Yes but humans can see sideways!) Human beings have four qualities that belong to the lower beings, animals: they eat and drink, procreate, excrete and die just like the animals (Genesis Rabbah 8.11).

So our human freedom can only be understood within the limitations that both these dimensions offer us. We are bounded and constrained by our nature as human beings.

The Rabbis taught: The philosophers asked the elders in Rome: If your God is unhappy that people pray to idols, why does He not simply destroy them? They replied: If they prayed to things that the world did not need, God would indeed have destroyed them. But they pray to the sun, moon, stars and planets. Should God destroy the world because of the actions of fools? The world pursues its natural course and fools who damage it will be held accountable. Another explanation: if someone stole a seah of corn and sowed it in the ground, according to the way of justice it ought not to sprout, but the world pursues its natural course, and the fools who damage it will be held accountable (Avodah Zarah 54b).

'The world pursues its natural course' and we are bound by our human nature no less than the rest of creation. Our freedom is limited long before we take on the shackles that human beings impose upon each other. In the phrase of Bob Dylan, 'Are birds free of the chains of the sky?' But birds do fly, and human beings do go about their daily activities subject to the laws of gravity. Our freedom exists, but within bounds imposed by the very nature of the world.

If nature is governed by laws of cause and effect, so too is there a divine law governing human behaviour in the biblical view. The problem is the unwillingness of human beings, and particularly Israel who should know better, to align themselves with it. Two biblical writers, Isaiah (28.24–28) and Jeremiah, made specific use of the term '*mishpat*'. We have examined it above in terms of 'law' or 'judgment' in the story of Abraham pleading for Sodom. But it also has the sense of the 'customary way' in which things happen (Gen. 40.13), and both prophets apply it to what they consider as an underlying regulating pattern within nature, an ultimate harmony of the universe to which all are subject.

Even the stork in the sky knows her season (to migrate)
and the dove and the swallow and the thrush keep to their time of coming, but My people do not know the '*mishpat*' of the Eternal (Jer. 8.7).

For the biblical writers God stands outside nature, so our own self-transcendence, our ultimate freedom, can only come from God. Anything less than that is simply another form of slavery.

For the children of Israel are slaves/servants to Me. My servants are they, whom I brought out of the land of Egypt. I am the Eternal your God' (Lev. 25.55).

And yet, even for the biblical writers it was not that simple. The psalmist can exclaim with wonder:

What is man that You remember him,
the son of man that You visit him?
Yet You have made him little less than divine,
crowning him with glory and honour! (Ps. 8.5).

But Job, out of his suffering, can turn the wonder at God's providence inside out:

What is man that You raise him,
that You set Your heart upon him,
visiting him every morning,
testing him every moment! (Job 7.17–18).

When the world goes right for us, God's attention may seem flattering. When it goes wrong the universe is not big enough to conceal us.

Where can I go from Your spirit
and where can I flee from Your presence.
If I ascend to heaven You are there,
or I make my bed in the underworld, there You are!
If I take the wings of the morning
and dwell in the farthest parts of the sea
there too Your hand shall lead me,
Your right hand grasp hold of me (Ps. 139.7–10).

As God enquired of Adam hiding in the garden after eating the forbidden fruit: 'ayekka', 'Where are you?' (Gen. 3.9). It is the question that echoes throughout the Bible. Every story is a variant on the same theme – the struggle between the will of God and that of the individual or group seeking their own independent destiny on their own terms. The cycles of stories about the patriarchs follow this pattern. As we have seen, had Abraham trusted God, Isaac would have been born to Sarah in God's own time. Instead Abraham tried to guarantee the result and Ishmael was born, only to be sent away so that Isaac could inherit. Two generations later Jacob received the Abrahamic blessing from his father Isaac on the point of being sent away in disgrace (Gen. 28.3–4). Stealing his brother's blessing merely caused him to spend twenty years in exile before he could return and take up his place. The children of Israel could have gone straight to their promised land without forty years in the wilderness, or could have stayed there forever without seventy years of exile in Babylon. The thrust of the biblical narrative is to address time and again this seeming paradox: the freedom granted to human beings and the desire on the part of God that they conform to the divine will, preferably from their own choice, but if not through threats and coercion. Each diversion from the path appointed by God has its consequences and lessons, but they too will become incorporated into the story as a whole when God's own plan somehow comes back on course. But that is also the price God has to pay for the freedom given to human beings to say no, to refuse to recognize where true freedom lies. God too is bounded by a covenant with willful humanity.

The Bible expresses this paradox of God's self-limited power through its stories and prophetic announcements. The Rabbis expressed it in their own way:

> Everything is foreseen, but freedom of choice is given (Pirqe Avot 3.15).

> Everything is in the hands of heaven except the fear of heaven (Berachot 33b, Megillah 25a, Niddah 16b).

Of course this freedom exists within certain natural boundaries over which we have no control:

> Against your will you are created, and against your will you are born, and against your will you live and against your will you die,

and against your will you will have to give an account and reckoning before the King above the kings of kings, the Holy One, blessed be He! (Pirqe Avot 4.22).

The Rabbis had their own solution to this riddle of the limitations and freedom of our existence. The revelation of God's teaching, the Torah, its study and its practice, provided the means to transcend our own limitations.

And the tablets were the work of God and the writing was the writing of God, inscribed ('charoot') upon the tablets (Ex. 32.16).

Do not read 'inscribed' ('charoot') but 'freedom' ('cheiroot'). For there is for you no freedom other than the engagement with Torah (Pirqe Avot 6.2).

And maybe that is where matters should be left. Except that religion was never that simple and human beings have always found ways to misuse it, as often as not to create their own new kinds of slavery. It is precisely here that the Bible is at its most subversive in challenging the very forms of religion that are dominant in its own society. In the days of Eli his sons tried to use the ark of the covenant as a magical talisman against their enemies – but found it to be utterly powerless (I Sam. 4.4–11). Jeremiah parodied those who saw the Temple as the magical answer to all their problems, 'who cry, "Temple of the Eternal! Temple of the Eternal! Temple of the Eternal!"' (Jer. 7.4). He lived to see the Temple destroyed as he had feared and warned. Neither Amos (4.4–5) nor Isaiah (1.10–17) were impressed with the holocausts of sacrifices made by their contemporaries out of religious zeal, when their behaviour was inexcusable. The willingness to critique the most central and fundamental religious institutions of their day, even at the cost of their own lives, was the legacy the prophets gave to the world. The Rabbis, in their own time, were no less sensitive to religious hypocrisy and also recognized how piety can lead to a distorted set of values:

Who is a pious fool? One who, if a woman is drowning, says, 'It is unseemly for me to look at her, so I cannot rescue her' (Sotah 21b).

Who is a pious fool? Someone who sees a child struggling in the
water and says, 'When I have taken off my *tefillin*, phylacteries, I
will go and save him', and while he is doing so the child drowns
(Jerusalem Talmud, Sotah 3.4).

The Rabbis were aware how easily religious zeal can be so
misplaced as to lead to violence and murder. In asking themselves
what were the grounds for the fight between Cain and Abel that led
to the latter's death, one opinion was:

Rabbi Joshua of Siknin said in the name of Resh Lakish:
. . . About what did they quarrel? Each demanded that the
Temple be built on his territory (Genesis Rabbah 22).

If freedom lies, in the biblical view, in seeking the nearness of
God, it is precisely at the point that we touch religion where the risk
most arises of getting it wrong, of becoming enslaved yet again. The
holiest place or tradition of one generation can become an idol for
the next. For Isaiah in his time Jerusalem was safe from the attack of
foreign invaders because God would not allow it to be destroyed. A
century later Jeremiah almost lost his life at the hands of the
authorities for warning that Jerusalem and the Temple were now
doomed. It is a hard biblical message: nothing is guaranteed forever
and, where God is concerned, nothing can ever be taken for
granted. The very attempt to pin God down to a time or a place, to a
ritual, a practice or a dogma, may be the first step towards disaster.
For it may become simply a way of re-making God in our own
image, of the creature seeking to control its creator, of putting
artificial limits on that which is unknowable. The god we can define
is no longer God.

They have a mouth but do not speak,
they have eyes but do not see.
They have ears but do not hear.
They have a nose but do not smell.
With their hands they do not feel,
with their feet they do not walk,
they make no sound in their throats.
Like them will be those that make them,
all who trust in them (Ps. 115.5–8).

Thus the opposite of liberation and freedom is ultimately idolatry.

God, as the supreme value and goal, is not man, the state, an institution, nature, power, possession, sexual powers, or any artifact made by man. The affirmations 'I love God', 'I follow God', 'I want to become like God' - mean first of all 'I do not love, follow or imitate idols.'

An idol represents the object of man's central passion: the desire to return to the soil-mother, the craving for possession, power, fame, and so forth. The passion represented by the idol is, at the same time, the supreme value within man's system of values. Only a history of idolatry could enumerate the hundreds of idols and analyze which human passions and desires they represent. May it suffice to say that the history of mankind up to the present time is primarily the history of idol worship, from the primitive idols of clay and wood to the modern idols of the state, the leader, production and consumption - sanctified by the blessing of an idolised God.[2]

To paraphrase the Passover message, just as each generation should consider themselves as if they personally had come out of Egypt and had stood at Sinai, so each person is duty bound to seek out and destroy the idols that enslave them.

The freedom that is won this way, within the biblical view, still operates within boundaries. It is a kind of freedom within community that will not tolerate the enslavement of others, whether through political or economic means, whether by emotional blackmail or through sheer brute force. In this sense the Exodus story, with its repeated retelling, is itself a kind of goad, forcing each new generation of readers to examine their own immediate society and the wider world around them, in the personal and collective sphere, in their institutions, the religious no less than the secular ones, and in the ideologies that dominate their thinking. For the enemy of freedom is idolatry and the prerequisite for idolatry is simply indifference or inertia. It is not enough simply to 'remember the Sabbath day' (Ex. 20.8), we must also 'keep' or 'guard' it (Deut. 5.12). Perhaps that is why the blessing recited each morning in Jewish tradition does not thank God for creating me 'free' but is expressed through a negative formulation. It is only through the constant remembrance of the slavery we must struggle against that we can value the freedom we have.

Blessed are You, our Living God, Sovereign of the universe, who has not made me a slave!

4

The 'Chosen People' and
the Peoples

It is one of the thorniest subjects that arises out of the Hebrew Bible, and one that has haunted the Jewish people over the millennia. Israel is the 'chosen people' in some sense – but what precisely that sense is and how it is understood within Israel and without remain controversial to this day. Perhaps it is true to say that however much Israel may have considered themselves to be in some way 'special', 'chosen by God' for a particular task, it is the outside world that has been obsessed with this idea. It has expressed itself in philosemitism and the expectation of 'higher standards' from the Jewish people, which might be flattering but often conceals a deadly kind of envy. The negative side, and infinitely more common, is antisemitism, a hatred of the Jewish people, that existed long before the specific term was invented in the nineteenth century and which culminated this century in genocide.

But what is Israel's perception of itself and its relation to God and the rest of the nations of the world? Since the origins of the people and their self-understanding are to be found in the Hebrew Bible, it is there that we must look in the first instance.

The biblical account expresses itself in a series of 'covenants', special contracts made between God and humanity. When the world that God created became corrupt God sought to destroy it by a flood, saving only one man Noah, and his family, in an ark which also rescued all the different species of animals. After the flood God made the first covenant with humanity as a whole which included the promise never to destroy the world again by a flood of water, symbolized by the presence of the rainbow in the sky.

The generations that descended from Noah, representing some seventy peoples (Gen. 10) populated the world, but remained as problematic as their predecessors. So God embarked on a new plan for their improvement, selecting one man, Abram/Abraham, testing him out rigorously, and only when convinced that he was right, giving him an offspring, Isaac. With Abraham God made the second covenant, promising his offspring their own land and a special role that would be of benefit to all of humanity, to be a blessing to all the families of the earth (Gen. 12.3). From Abraham are to descend Isaac, then Jacob whose twelve sons were to found twelve tribes, the basis of a new nation. But before the stage of nation-building could take place they had to experience exile and slavery in the land of Egypt.

No reason is given for this enslavement in the Bible, though God warns Abraham that it will happen to his descendants (Gen. 15.13). (Though it is not relevant to the theme of this particular chapter, it is worth recording one Rabbinic view that relates to the last chapter. The children of Rachel and Leah, Jacob's 'true' wives, used to mock the children of Bilhah and Zilpah, their handmaidens – saying that unlike themselves, they were only the children of 'slaves'. As a lesson, God decreed that all the descendants of Jacob should experience slavery so that the distinctions between them would be removed; all would be the children of slaves!)

Following the liberation from Egypt under the leadership of Moses, Israel encounters God at Mt Sinai and enters into the third covenant, this time between God and the entire people. It is here that the nature, and something of the purpose, of this special relationship is spelled out. In speaking to Moses as the intermediary in the negotiation that is to follow, God addresses Israel in the following terms:

> You have seen what I have done to Egypt. How I lifted you up on eagles' wings and brought you to Me. So now, if you will surely listen to/obey My voice and keep My covenant, then you will be special to Me from all the peoples, for all the earth is Mine. And you shall be to Me a kingdom of priests and a holy nation. These are the things you are to tell to the children of Israel (Ex. 19.4–6).

A special role is to be undertaken by this people, chosen by a God who owns all the earth and is therefore free to make such a choice. The precise sense of the task is not clear. A priest has a special relationship with God, so in this sense Israel are to be the priests that represent humanity to God, but must also ensure that the world fulfills its spiritual duties. In this sense Israel is intimately related to the rest of humanity and bears a kind of responsibility for it. However the second term, 'a holy nation', emphasizes the 'otherness' and isolation of Israel – the term 'holy', *qadosh*, bearing the sense of separation, apartness. In some extraordinary way this invitation came to be a self-fulfilling hypothesis in that it accurately reflects the ambivalent situation of Israel and subsequently the Jewish people as indicated earlier. For the time being, within the Book of Exodus, the negotiation has to continue, with the people accepting in principle God's offer and then hammering out the details as the Ten Commandments and a further series of detailed laws (Ex. 21–23) which make up the conditions of accepting the covenant, are spelled out. In short, Israel is to create a special kind of society on the territory that God is to give to them. This society, if it can be made to work, is then to become a model for the rest of humanity.

The rest of the Hebrew Bible in some way reflects the working out of this covenant hope – its successes but more often its failures. In the remainder of this chapter we will look more specifically at some aspects of the nature of this society and how it is seen to relate to the rest of the nations of the world.

Though Abraham has his origins in the Mesopotamian world, the cradle of the new society is Egypt, one of the major powers in the Ancient Near East. Israel acquired much of its culture from both these two ancient centres of civilization. Its physical location between them, in the small area of territory that controlled the great highways for trade, commerce and military movement meant that while sometimes it could exert its independence, for the most part it existed in a vassal situation between the two. Thus Israel early developed a sophisticated understanding of the *real politik* of the area, in terms of the small states that made up that territory and the great empires that took it in turns to control it. Israel had to understand and play its part in the world merely to survive.

Egypt

Divide and conquer   It would be hard to overestimate the importance of Egypt in Israelite consciousness for the biblical writers. The story of the Exodus, as well as being central to the Israelite understanding of their origins, becomes a model for interpreting the

Babylonian exile and the return. The remembrance of Egyptian slavery becomes a crucial concept underlying the legislation concerned not only with the treatment of slaves, but of all resident aliens and all vulnerable social groups in their territory. The later history of the divided kingdoms (Judah in the south, Israel in the north) is intimately bound up with the political vicissitudes of the regional 'superpowers'. Though alliances with Egypt were attacked by the prophets, this antagonism relates to a distrust of any such political dependencies and a scepticism about the reliability of Egypt as an ally. There is almost none of the anger and hatred that sometimes characterize the views of Assyria and Babylon. The memory and depiction of Egypt is thus surprisingly sympathetic despite it being the 'house of slaves' from which they saw themselves as having emerged.

The Book of Exodus is either a source of this attitude or a reflection of it, depending on one's view of the historical development of these texts.

As we have seen above, the instructions in the Bible to 'teach your children' about the events of the Exodus (Ex. 10.2; 12.26; 13.8, 14) will subsequently lie at the heart of the elaborate Passover festival, thus reinforcing the feeling that each detail of what happened is enormously important. The Exodus events are important in broad theological terms (God's intervention in human history and concern with the fate of Israel) and in terms of the set of human values they instill (freedom from slavery, 'liberation'). But in the first instance the story portrays the political negotiations between Pharaoh and Moses.

It is vital to notice from the outset that the Egyptians are not depicted as uniformly wicked, nor, for that matter, are the Israelites all good, or, at least, instantly faithful to their God. A Pharaoh is the instigator of events and his successor continues his policies, but his officers and the Egyptian people in general are represented as distinct from him and finally in opposition to his actions. It is that sort of discrimination that must be borne in mind when evaluating the overall view of Egypt.

The story begins with the dramatic announcement of the 'arising' of a new king over Egypt who did not know Joseph. The use of the terminology of 'a new king' has long suggested the possibility that this marked a dynastic change, though attempts to pin down the exact historical date remain the subject of debate. In such a situation the wider implications of the new king 'knowing' or 'not knowing' Joseph become clearer – the refusal to 'acknowledge' the power or position or legitimacy of an appointee of the previous regime and his successors. This sense of the word is reinforced when we follow the use of this same hebrew verb *yada* throughout this section. Not only does Pharaoh 'not know' Joseph, his successor, as we have already seen, will not *know* the God of the Hebrews (Ex. 5.2) and part of the intention of the plagues will be the frequently stated purpose to make sure that Pharaoh and the Egyptians do come to *know* God (Ex. 7.5; 8.6, 18; 9.14, 29; 11.7; 14.4, 18). This reminds us that in addition to the national or particularistic purpose of the Exodus in God's scheme, it also has a conscious universalistic purpose, and that both of these elements were equally emphasized in Israel's understanding of its origins.

We are dealing with the politics of a new power structure. In such circumstances the approach to the Israelites, as recorded in the first chapter of Exodus, becomes clearer.

[Pharaoh] said to his people: 'Behold the people, the children of Israel, are greater and more powerful than we. Come let us deal wisely with them lest they increase and when war approaches us, they will also join with our enemies and fight against us and go up from the land' (Ex. 1.9–10).

The overt reason for concern about them, their increasing numerical strength and the risk that they will become a fifth column, may well reflect some political reality, but is nevertheless very close in tone to the scaremongering tactics of demagogues throughout history. The Bible records one other such ploy which nearly led to a vast destruction when Haman incited King Ahsasuerus against the Jews living in his realms:

There is a certain people scattered abroad and dispersed among the peoples in all the provinces of your kingdom; their laws are different from those of every other people, and they do not keep the king's laws, so that it is not for the king's profit to tolerate them. If it please the king let it be decreed that they be destroyed, and I will pay ten thousand talents of silver into the hands of those who have charge of the king's business, that they may put it into the king's treasuries (Esther 3.8–9).

Such ploys have been used throughout history by regimes seeking a scapegoat to help secure their own position of power. Even the phraseology, 'come let us deal wisely with them' (Ex. 1.10) and the subsequent plot hatched by Pharaoh suggest a secret and unprovoked assault upon a people not otherwise considered as a threat by the general populace.

I have recorded elsewhere[1] the commentary on the events that follow by Nachmanides (Rabbi Moshe ben Nachman, 'RaMBaN' 1194–1270), but they bear repetition:

> Pharaoh and his counsellors did not want to slay them by the sword for it would have been a great treachery to smite for no reason a people admitted to the land by command of a previous king. Furthermore, the people of the land would not allow the king to do a violent act like that, for he was accustomed to consult with them, and all the more so since the children of Israel were a numerous and mighty people and would fight a great war against them. But he said that he would employ wisdom so that Israel would not feel that he was acting with enmity against them.
>
> It is for that reason that he imposed a levy on them, it being a custom for resident aliens to pay a levy to the king, as happened in the reign of King Solomon. Then afterwards he instructed the midwives in secret to kill the male children on the birthstool, so that even the mothers themselves would not know it. Then after that he instructed his people: 'Every male child that is born you shall cast into the Nile' (Ex. 1.22) you yourselves. In essence he did not want to command his executioners to kill them with the sword of the king or to throw them into the Nile, but rather he told the people, whoever should find a Jewish child he should throw it into the Nile. And if the father of the child should complain to the king or the head of the city he would respond by asking him to provide witnesses so that he could punish the crime. Now when the king's strap was removed (i.e. the usual restrictions on injustice were set aside in the case of the Israelites), the Egyptians were free to search out houses and to enter them by night and with complete unconcern (lit. making themselves strangers) take the children out from there (Nachmanides on Ex. 1.10).

There are chilling similarities between Nachmanides' reading and the stages whereby the Nazis first disenfranchised, then gradually robbed their Jewish citizens of their status as human beings, thus freeing people from any sense of remorse about mistreating them. Other commentators increase the stages of this subjugation by seeing in 1.11–14 a gradual worsening of the work to which they were subjected with its subsequent degradation.

A further stage of subjugation is created in which Egyptian taskmasters employ Israelite 'foremen' to rule over their fellow Israelite slaves (Ex. 5.14). This is a familiar policy of divide and conquer, of alienating one particular class from the rest of the populace by giving them a higher status and making them dependent on the ruling power both to maintain their position and protect them from the anger of their own people. An additional effect is to provide a buffer group between the subjugated and those who wield the real power. The biblical account provides in brief but clear images a sharp picture of a hierarchical, repressive regime. Whether it accords with a 'real', recoverable Egyptian society may be difficult to assess, but from the point of view of the narrative that was to become scripture, this is part of the 'truth' of the Egyptian bondage.

The Pharaoh who deals with the returning Moses is no less a subtle political animal than his predecessor. When confronted by Moses' initial demand, in addition to dismissing this unknown 'god', he proceeds to undermine this potentially dangerous new leadership by increasing substantially the burden of the work and hinting that it is all because of the dangerous initiative of Moses. He does this in part by twice quoting Moses' own words, the second time rubbing it in (compare 5.17 and 5.8 with 5.3). This further policy of divide and conquer seems to prove successful as indicated by the bitter greeting Moses receives from the foremen (5.21).

These precise distinctions between the various participants in the story are very important and should not be glossed over. Because with God's response through the plagues a process is initiated in which Pharaoh in turn is gradually separated from different sections of his own society and ultimately isolated. The same ploy of divide and conquer comes back against him. If that represents the inner political strategy of God against Pharaoh, its broader lesson for the Israelites is to recognize differentiated groups among the Egyptians. It is to these fine distinctions that they are to respond and there can be no single wicked 'Egypt' as the focus of hatred and prejudice.

The plagues   The narrative about the plagues is very carefully constructed around a recurrent threefold pattern. In each cycle, the first plague is announced by a warning to Pharaoh in the morning (blood, swarms, hail); the second in each cycle is also preceded by a warning (frogs, pestilence, locusts); the third in each cycle has no warning before it (gnats, boils, darkness). The three plagues in each cycle become progressively more unpleasant and the three cycles themselves become progressively more sinister, the first group making life unpleasant and uncomfortable, the second group causing sickness and damage, the third group causing danger to life, and death.

Within that pattern various other sequences work themselves out. One major topic is the magicians of Pharaoh. In the contest as it is set up, Moses stands in oppostion to Pharaoh (a 'god' against another 'god') while Aaron, as his 'prophet' (7.1) and agent in ushering in some of the plagues, plays a role equivalent to the magicians.

These various magical acts may appear as no more than conjuring tricks, but they represent a challenge that goes to the heart of Egyptian religion and culture. They are an assault on the sources of power of that vast society with its slave economy, with its huge building projects, its technological expertise, its enormous bureaucracy, its rich cultural and artistic heritage. More precisely, the 'magicians' are the privileged 'technocrats' of that world because of their special skills. As Sarna explains:

Egypt, especially, was the classic land of magic, which played a central role in its religious life . . . Human destiny was thought to be controlled by two distinct forces, the gods and the powers beyond the gods. Neither of these was necessarily benevolent. In fact, antagonism and malevolence were considered to be characteristic of the divine relationship with man. Inevitably, religion became increasingly concerned with the elaboration of ritual designed to propitiate or neutralize the numerous unpredictable powers that be . . . The magician was an important, indeed indispensable, religious functionary. He possessed the expertise necessary for the manipulation of the mysterious powers . . .

In the light of all this, the performance of signs and wonders in Egypt on the part of Moses, and the high concentration of this motif in the story of the Exodus, admirably suit the social and religious milieu. Yet appearances are deceptive. While the actions of Moses appear to belong to the same category as those of the Egyptian practitioners, in actual fact the comparison is superficial.[2]

As the Exodus narrative develops, the power of the magicians is diminished and shown to be absurd against the real power of Israel's God. The stages are clear: they can reproduce the snakes (Ex. 7.10–12); the Nile water turning to blood is also within their competence (7.22), but that ability to reproduce what is essentially a plague is already absurd. Like the sorcerer's apprentice, the one thing they cannot do is reverse the disasters. They can similarly reproduce the frogs (8.7) but again merely adding to the disaster.

Their first real admission of defeat comes with the third plague, gnats, when they describe the event with which they cannot compete as *etzba elohim*, the 'finger of God' (8.19). But it is not clear what is the precise nuance of this phrase. Is it an acknowledgment of a divine intercession or is the term *elohim* (god) being used here in the more general sense of the phrase *yirat elohim*, 'the fear of God', as in Gen. 20.11, where it means, in very broad terms, moral or ethical values? (The same sense may also apply to the 'fear of God' of the midwives (Ex. 1.17) – they have a moral sense.) Thus the 'finger of God' could have more or less the same sense as 'an act of god' in an insurance policy, a natural disaster beyond human control, but not yet evidence of a direct, causal intervention by God, and certainly not Israel's YHWH. Their statement would thus be a face-saving gesture before Pharaoh.

But they are not allowed to get away with this evasion. The plague of boils will actually touch them physically to the extent that they can no longer even enter the lists with Moses (9.11). Here we see the 'extrinsic subversive' mode of the Bible operating at its most ironic.

A new element enters with the fourth plague, variously translated as 'swarms of flies' or of 'wild beasts'. In this case the land of Goshen where the Israelites live is separated off and unaffected (8.23, 25). This separation will be repeated in the cattle plague of 9.4, the hail (9.26) and the darkness (10.21). This degree of discrimination moves the events beyond a natural cataclysm into a precise divine intervention, something the magicians have tried to deny.

From now on, as well, separate Egyptian groups will become more differentiated. Some of the 'servants' of Pharaoh accept Moses' word and take their cattle in to protect them from the hail (10.20). Before the plague of locusts they will start to argue with Pharaoh to let the Israelites go. As Pharaoh becomes more isolated his bargaining options diminish and his obsession seems to grow.

From this point Egypt becomes less and less a real place or nation and only the power-hungry obsessiveness of its leader remains. It is one of the achievements of the narrative that the more God's power becomes manifest, the greater our sympathy grows for the Eyptian people themselves, trapped within a system that gives such absolute power to their leader.

The final plague steps out of the system of threes that has preceded it and by its very horror breaks also the pattern of graded severity that has appeared in each of the three cycles. The fact that the first-born alone are killed suggests that this is no arbitrary choice. On one level it may represent a measure for measure punishment for the slaying of the Israelite male children as attempted by the Pharaoh at the onset of the story. On another it gives an aetiological background to the role to be played by the first-born in Israel that are dedicated to God (13.11–16), and who will in turn be superseded by the Levites.

Israelite society/Egyptian society   Israel's experience in Egypt functions as an 'anti-model' for the society Israel was to create. How far it is possible to distinguish political realities from the theological narrative that contains them remains an insoluble problem, but the following set of associations make a very powerful condemnation of the image of Egyptian society Israel opposed.

Genesis 47 relates the consequences of the famine which Pharaoh's dreams had predicted. Joseph, with full state support, had filled the store cities during the seven years of plenty. Now the seven years of famine had begun to bite and Joseph was approached by people seeking food. As the text narrates, in successive years they paid for it with their money (47.14) and their cattle (47.16–17), and ultimately offered their bodies and their land (18–21, 23) to Pharaoh in return for food.

There is something very poignant in their desperation when they plead, v. 19, 'we ourselves and our land shall be slaves to Pharaoh'. The land and the people are to become the property of Pharaoh and the entire nation is reduced to slave status. In contrast to this the Israelite alternative is to acknowledge that all human beings are indeed 'slaves', but 'slaves' not to any human power, but to God alone. Indeed at the heart of the struggle between Pharaoh and Moses are two utterly different perceptions of the term *eved* (slave/servant). In Pharaoh's Egypt, a slave is the lowest form of human existence. In Moses' terminology, to be a 'slave of YHWH' is the highest freedom (7.16 etc.). It is as the 'slave of YHWH' that he is designated at his death (Deut. 34.5).

With regard to the treatment of slaves, the model of Egyptian cruelty is consciously opposed. In Ex. 1.13, 14, the Egyptians 'made them serve *b'farech*, with rigour'. The same word recurs repeatedly as a direct prohibition in the Jubilee legislation about the treatment and release of slaves: 'You shall not rule over him *b'farech*, with rigour (Lev. 25.43, 46, 53). Significantly, also, the first legislation recorded after the giving of the Ten Commandments, which is presumably meant to be the first set of laws of the covenant itself, is the law limiting the period of slavery to six years. Once again the social lessons to be drawn from the Egyptian experience have been separated from any emotional feelings against Egypt and instead have entered into Israel's legislative structure.

What is astonishing about the record of the Egyptian experience in Exodus and then elsewhere in the Hebrew Bible is the sympathy that is retained for the Egyptians despite the suffering and horror contained within the events. From the experience of slavery there are lessons to be drawn – about giving rest to your own servants and about the proper treatment of your own Hebrew slaves and of the 'stranger' within your territory. Your Israelite society is meant to express a total contrast with that of Egypt. But nevertheless the Israelites should not despise an Egyptian, because you were settlers with them once; moreover, unlike the case of the Moabites and Ammonites, an Egyptian may enter the house of Israel after the third generation (Deut. 23.8–9).

Perhaps the roots of this familiarity are already expressed within the Exodus narrative itself as we have seen in the last chapter. The rescuer of Moses, the future saviour and creator of the nation, is Pharaoh's daughter. The 'Hebrew midwives' might be either Israelites or Egyptian 'midwives of the Hebrews', and are probably the latter.

Similarly towards the end of the story comes the episode of leave-taking and the presents pressed on the Israelites by their Egyptian neighbours. There are questions about what precisely happened – did Israel 'borrow' under false pretenses or 'ask for' what everyone knew would not be returned? That God gave the Israelites favour in the eyes of the Egyptians is clearly stated (Ex. 11.3; 12.36). More problematic is the phrase that Israel 'despoiled the Egyptians' (12.36), variously understood as they 'stripped' them, or 'emptied them out'. This can be seen as either evidence of a triumphal departure or a final revenge (to be later paid for in the ornaments that went to build the Golden Calf!) or as the acquiring of wages for several centuries' unpaid labour, on the lines of Israel's own laws about what was to be paid to a slave on his release:

> When you set him free do not let him go empty-handed. Load him up with what you take from the flock, threshing floor and vat with which the Eternal your God has blessed you. Remember that you were a slave in the land of Egypt and the Eternal your God redeemed you; therefore I command you this thing today (Deut. 15.13–15).

But there is another way entirely to read the verb here translated as 'spoil'. In its commoner form it is used of 'snatching' someone out of danger, of 'rescuing'. The same verbal form occurs in Ezekiel:

> Even if these three men, Noah, Daniel and Job, were in (the land) they, with all their righteousness, would only be able to *rescue* themselves . . . (Ezek. 14.14).

By this reading, the Israelites 'saved' the Egyptians by claiming their wages or by accepting presents from them so that they parted in the final moment as friends.

Whether this final interpretation is true to this immediate text is hard to say. Nevertheless what does emerge here is the surprising sympathy felt for the Egyptians within the Exodus narrative, the Hebrew Bible as a whole and in later Jewish tradition. From the various elements we have uncovered it seems clear that the Exodus 'saved' Israelites and Egyptians alike. The achievement of the narrator/s has been to transform what might have been a mere triumphalist account of an enemy vanquished and freedom gained into a multi-layered symbolic struggle between two concepts of the human-divine relationship and two understandings of human society that derive from them. It is that universal significance that makes the Exodus narrative a touchstone and a penetrating challenge for individuals and societies alike until today.

The nations of the world

The Hebrew Bible presents itself as history: from the creation of the world itself, through the appearance of different peoples and nations to the emergence of one particular people, the descendants of Abraham, Isaac and Jacob. Throughout the detailed account of Israel's development from families to tribes to an enslaved people to a nation on their own territory, through empire, divided kingdoms, exile and return, this drama is acted out on the world stage. For the biblical writers, however much they may concentrate on the detailed inner experiences of Israel, this broader background is assumed, and indeed the interaction with local nation states and the contemporary great empires of Egypt, Assyria and Babylon is crucial at all stages of this history.

The biblical perception of humanity is framed by the Genesis account of the creation of the first human being who is the ancestor of all human beings. Therefore all individuals and peoples share the same heritage of being created in the image of God. Israel's history as a nation can only be understood against the background of the other nations of the world. We have seen above the two-fold nature of the relationship between Israel and the other nations as envisaged in the covenant at Sinai. In this formulation the twin poles of Israel's nature and experience are spelled out, its simultaneous universalism and particularism, either aspect of which may be emphasized at any time.

This tension is affected both by internal and external situations, but even the narrowest concerns of biblical Israel are acted out on this world stage. Thus at times it is possible to see Israel's history depicted as a private conversation between Israel and God with the surrounding peoples and nations as mere onlookers or occasional bit-players, sent to punish an errant Israel that is temporarily disobeying God. But at the same time, particularly in the prophetic writings, the other nations are also granted their independent significance and responsibility. God is seen as intervening in their history as well, whether they are aware of this or not. The prophet

Amos emphasizes this when challenging Israel's feeling of uniqueness before God:

> Did I not bring Israel up of Egypt, the Philistines from Caphtor and the Arameans from Kir? (Amos 9.7).

God has intervened in the sacred history and migrations of all peoples in exactly the same way as with Israel.

Yet what is this people and how does it relate to God? One starting point is the actual terminology used in the Hebrew Bible to describe the Israelite people or nation. Two words are commonly used, neither of them with great precision, and quite often they seem to be interchangeable. The words are *goi* and *'am*. The former, *goi*, is a term used both of Israel and of the other nations, often referred to in the plural, *goyim*. It seems to be the word which defines a nation in terms of its basis in political or territorial unity or common ancestry.[3] The word *'am* is used more frequently to indicate a people linked through their common ancestry, while *goi* stresses the territorial aspect and a common language, but the terms are not used exclusively so. The one distinction, however, that is made between them is that with regards Israel, only *'am* is used in connection with the name of God either referring to 'the people of YHWH' or, with the personal pronoun, as 'My people', or 'Your people'.

Martin Buber sees a particular distinction between the terms:

> One people must set an example of harmony in obedience to God for the others. From a mere nation, from the biological and historical unity of a *goi* . . ., it must become a community, a true *am* whose members are connected not merely by origin and common lot, but are also bound to one another by just and loving participation in a common life. But it can do this only as an *am elohim*, a people of God, in which all are bound to one another through their common tie to a divine centre. A pseudo-community which lacks the centre (Gen. 11.6) [the Tower of Babel] must fall apart. For men become brothers only as they become children of one Father. That fratricide [Cain's killing of Abel] and that building of the Tower can only be atoned for and overcome together.[4]

Another way of understanding this distinction between the words relates to their expressing a nearness to or distance from God. For example, after the episode of the Golden Calf, when Moses is pleading with God to remain with the people on their journey through the wilderness, Moses lets slip a bit of his own exasperation in trying to lead such a difficult people: *ki am'cha ha-goi ha-zeh* – 'for *Your* people is this nation!'

Whether the people belongs to Moses or to God is the subject of a curious dialogue between God and Moses, also after the episode of the Golden Calf. In telling Moses what the people have done, God very pointedly refers to them as '*your* people whom *you* brought out from the land of Egypt . . . I have seen this people and it is a stiff-necked people' (Ex. 32.7, 9). God threatens to destroy them and create a new '*goi*' based on Moses himself (32.10). Moses seeks to appease God by saying: 'Why, O Eternal, should Your anger be hot against *Your* people whom *You* brought up from the land of Egypt . . .' (v. 11).

The distinction between *goi* and *'am* appears again in a saying of the prophet Isaiah, also a reflection of divine anger. Here it is possible that the two terms are simply parallel, but the sequence of words would point to something different. The Hebrew has a power of its own: *hoi goi hotei – am keved avon – zera m're'im – banim mashhitim* – 'Shame on a nation that strays – a people weighed down with sin – offspring that do evil – children that destroy!' (Isa. 1.4). The words that describe the people move from more distant ones to closer ones: 'nation – people – offspring – children'. However, the terms for describing their wrongdoing get progressively stronger: straying – sinning – doing evil – destroying. The closer the sense of relationship the greater the sense of betrayal.

If God is prepared to chastise Israel through the words of the prophets, they are equally willing to criticize the behaviour of the other nations as well. However in doing so it seems that the prophets always have their own people in mind. Alongside the concern for establishing values that should be universally applied, there is always a particular message for Israel. An example of this can be found in the opening chapters of Amos. It is clear from the sequence of nations that are addressed by the prophet that his aim is not merely to chastise them, but to use this rhetorical technique as a way of addressing the real target of his criticism, the Northern Kingdom of Israel itself. By getting their agreement to his attack on the others, the prophet softens up his audience for the moment when he narrows in on them. And indeed it is not clear in the case of

all the 'oracles against the nations' in prophetic writings how far
these were addressed to the nations in question and indeed
delivered to them, and how far they were rhetorical devices for the
sake of having an impact on Israel itself.

It is instructive to look in some detail at Amos' words, each
beginning with the formula: 'For the three sins of X, even for four, I
will not turn it back . . . (the "it" probably being punishment)'.[5]
Syria is criticized for violent cross-border incursions (1.3); Gaza,
the Philistine city on the coast, for deporting people and selling
them as slaves; the same criticism applies to the northern port of
Tyre but adds that by doing so they were breaking their ancient
covenant treaty with Israel. The above three are neighbouring
peoples who have no ties of kinship with Israel. The criticisms
belong in the political arena and reflect the sort of grievances that
arise between neighbouring states that live in uneasy relationship
with each other. They would have had a sympathetic hearing from
his Israelite audience, allowing them to take the moral high ground.
Nevertheless, the criticisms represent abuse of general principles
governing the relations between nations.

Next Amos turns to Edom, from the biblical point of view a
people descended from Esau, the twin brother of Jacob, therefore
with closer 'family' ties. But in this case old causes of anger are
evoked harking back to Edom's refusal to allow Israel right of
passage through their land during the wilderness period and
threatening to fight them (Num. 20.14–21). Beyond even that there
is a reminder of Jacob's betrayal of Esau over the firstborn blessing,
something that Esau's descendants have never forgotten:

> for pursuing their brother with the sword and suppressing their
> compassion and for keeping their anger forever (1.11).

The sequence, as well as going from more 'distant' neighbours in
a kinship sense, has also been circling round the country, from
north-east to south-west, to north-west to due south. Now we come
to the two nations on the other side of the Jordan river, Ammon and
Moab, traditionally seen as sons of Lot, Abraham's nephew,
through an incestuous act with his two daughters. Ammon is
criticized for disembowelling pregnant women during raids to
extend their border with Israel (1.13). Moab is criticized for burning
the bones of the King of Edom (2.1). These latter two are
perplexing till one realizes that they address an assault on the

sacredness of life itself – destroying those not yet born and desecrating the bodies of the dead.

The prophet now comes even closer to home, attacking the Southern Kingdom of Judah, the other half of the Israelite nation but in so many ways its rival. His critique has to do with their abuse of the inner regulations of the covenant with God. They have despised and abandoned the Torah and commandments of God and pursued idols. Since these are views commonly held by his audience in the Northern Kingdom, he has by now utterly won over their sympathy. Then he unleashes a precise attack on their own economic injustice and exploitation of the poor:

> for selling the innocent party in a court case for silver and the poor for a pair of shoes; for panting after the very dust on the head of the poor and perverting the justice due to the needy; a father and son will share the same woman so as to defile God's holy name; they lie out on clothes held in pledge next to their altars and drink confiscated wine in the House of their God (2.6–8).

Though in this particular instance the criticism works from outwards in, from foreign nations to the heart of the Israelite community, certain universal principles are evoked. The sacredness of life, the integrity of borders, the demand for justice as a basis for any society, the condemnation of the exploitation of the poor and weak, all of which are seen as a reflecting on the honour due to God. It is justice and integrity that are the cement that holds together the life of a people and the family of nations as well.

Amos' point of reference is the nations that form Israel's immediate neighbours and the local issues that affect them. Other prophets, notably Isaiah and Jeremiah, reflect on a broader stage of the great world empires of their time. But their criticism is no less precise and harsh. What lies behind their words is a perception of a world under the ultimate guidance of one God. However the different nations may perceive their own gods and their power, this principle of ultimate unity takes on a logic of its own. If humanity were created by God as a single pair, if all the nations descended from one survivor of the flood, then the possibility of a return to some kind of international unity under God is there. And if not in the immediate present then in the not-too-distant future.

This expectation is celebrated in Isaiah's famous vision of all nations flowing to Zion to learn God's teaching (Isa. 2.3). Here too it is important to recognize that the 'Torah that comes from Zion' is not merely a theoretical system of values, for God will 'judge between the nations and reprove many peoples'. The establishment of universal justice is the essential prelude to the beating of swords into ploughshares so that 'nation will not lift up sword against nation, nor ever again train for war'. The end is human unity and harmony. In that time, Israel will take its place in a world not different from the present, because the nations will still be there in their distinctiveness. But they will be united under the rule of the One God:

> On that day will Israel be a third with Egypt and Assyria as a blessing in the midst of the earth in that the Eternal One of hosts will bless it, saying: Blessed be My people Egypt and the work of My hands Assyria and My inheritance, Israel (Isa. 19.24–25).

Messianic hopes and political realities

It would be nice to be able to end here with a tidy and comfortable biblical view of harmonious nations and messianic hopes. But though such hopes are present, the Hebrew Bible focusses time and again on the reality of international conflicts, wars of conquest and defence, the movements of imperial armies across bloodstained landscapes. And there are alliances, treaties, rebellions, betrayals, war crimes and rallying cries that amount to genocide. The Bible does not invent wars of extermination or ethnic cleansing, but it knows of their existence in the behaviour of the nations and empires around Israel, and in the actions, or at least the ideology, of biblical Israel itself.

Though the versions of the conquest of the land in Joshua and Judges are mutually contradictory. they must reflect a protracted and violent process of settlement. It was the men who fought such wars on a hand-to-hand basis, so the aim was to kill as many men capable of bearing arms as possible. Any that survived could fight you again on a later occasion. But the other victims of wars, particularly border disputes, were women and children. If captured they could become part of the conqueror's spoil and property. Otherwise they would have to be killed, especially pregnant women, as they represented the next generation of enemy fighters. These realities are never far away from the biblical view of the world.

But alongside the accounts of Israel's struggles that are presented as history in the books from Joshua to Kings, there is a 'theological' approach presented in the Book of Deuteronomy. It presents itself as Moses' final speech, but seems to reflect a much later period, long after the settlement. It contains in a few brief sentences the cruellest of commands to exterminate those who belonged to the seven nations that inhabited Canaan and destroy all traces of their religious worship (Deut. 7.1–11; 20.16–18). But in the same context Deuteronomy also provides guidelines on the humane conduct of war. When besieging a town peace terms must be offered and only if refused should a war to the finish take place (Deut. 20.10f.). A scorched earth policy was forbidden – all fruit-bearing trees were to be preserved (Deut. 20.19). A distinction appears to be made (at least according to later Rabbinic interpretation) between wars of defense when all Israelites may be recruited and wars for political purposes or to gain territory (20.15) when exemptions were made for all those in the process of building their family, home or land.

The inhabitants belonging to the seven nations were to come under a ban. The term for it, *herem*, is a difficult one because it ranges in meaning from simply confiscating and destroying all the possessions of the captured people and avoiding any contacts with them, to utterly destroying them in the name of a divine command.

It has to be pointed out that these texts in Deuteronomy seem to come from a time long after the conquest was over. They can only have been theoretical as far as the seven nations are concerned and perhaps belong to a kind of triumphalist liturgy. Nevertheless they are there in the Hebrew Bible and available to be quoted by those who want to justify their own murderous activities.

Rabbinic responses to these verses are odd. One passage has God angry with Israel because of the fact that it did *not* utterly destroy the Hittites and Amorites. The proof they bring of this failure is the fact that Joshua spared Rahab the harlot, who had saved the life of Joshua's spies, together with her family in Jericho. But the 'punishment' Israel is to receive because of this is actually a backhanded compliment from God. According to Rabbinic tradition, Rahab converted to Judaism and one of her descendants was the prophet Jeremiah, one of the strongest critics of Israel's behaviour:

> Behold, the prophet Jeremiah will spring from the children's children of Rahab the harlot and will thrust such words into you as will be thorns in your eyes and pricks in your sides (Pesikta De-Rab Kahana 13.5).[6]

The Rabbinic midrash on Deuteronomy, Sifre,[7] does attempt to soften the violence. Thus if Canaanites of the seven nations are in the cities that accept peace terms, they are not to be harmed (Piska 200). The Rabbis also focussed on the reason given by Deuteronomy for destroying the local population, because they will 'teach you to do after all their abominations' (Deut. 20.18). This means, the Rabbis argued, that if they repent of their idolatry and accept Israel's God, so that they do not lead Israel astray, they are not to be slain (Piska 202). In the case of a city that refused to accept peace terms, once they had conquered it, according to Deuteronomy the Israelites are commanded to slay all the males (Deut. 20.13), but by a careful argument the Rabbis managed to exclude all minors from this category, even if they had fought against Israel (Piska 200).

The Talmud records a Rabbinic formulation that effectively removed all such passages from consideration. A verse in Deuteronomy (23.4) states that an Ammonite and Moabite may not enter into the community of the Eternal even to the tenth generation. On this Rabbi Joshua points out that since the days when Sennacherib came and confused all the nations, by deporting them and resettling their land with other populations, no one could identify the original inhabitants of the land any more (Berakhot 28a). If this applied to the Ammonites and Moabites it must have applied to all the other inhabitants of the area who had been subjected to the same experience.

One other nation is singled out for particular consideration. After Israel safely crossed the Sea of Reeds they were attacked by a people called Amalek (Ex. 17.8–16). The Israelites defeated them, and God tells Moses of an oath: 'I will surely blot out the memory of Amalek from under the heavens.' Moses constructs an altar there and makes an oath: 'A hand upon the throne of God! There will be war between God and Amalek in every generation!'

Why Amalek is singled out for this action is not clear from the passage in Exodus. However the account is elaborated in Deuteronomy. Amalek fell on the rear of the Israelite march where the weakest people were to be found, those who were tired and weary. It adds: 'and they did not fear God'. As we suggested above this is a biblical idiom meaning 'they had no moral sense'.[8] On this reading their deed was not simply an act of war, but was a cowardly attack on those who were utterly defenceless. Here the command of God is to 'blot out the memory of Amalek from under the sun' (Deut. 25.17–19). Two other biblical texts in particular deal with Amalek. The prophet Samuel tells King Saul to destroy the Amalekites, but having defeated them Saul spares them and their property. It is this disobedience that leads God to depose Saul as king (I Sam. 15). In the Book of Esther, Haman, the man who tries to exterminate the Jews, is an Agagite, a descendant of the king of Amalek spared by Saul. Since Mordechai who defeats Haman is a member of Saul's family, the Book of Esther is, at least on one level, a replay of that previous encounter and an attempt to correct Saul's failure and to blot out the name of Amalek.

So who is Amalek? They are not mentioned in any extra-biblical source. According to Genesis (36.11–12) Amalek was a descendant of Esau. They seem to have been semi-nomadic people living on the fringe of areas where settled populations could be found, settlements that they frequently raided. In the historical books Israel was to do battle with them at various times (Num. 14.43–45; Jud. 3.13; 6.3–5, 33; 7.12; 10.12; I Sam. 27.6; 30.1–20) where they acted alone or in alliance with other enemies of Israel. The Book of Chronicles records that 'only a remnant of the Amalekites' was left at the time of King Hezekiah (I Chron. 4.43).

But for Deuteronomy they have clearly taken on a kind of mythic significance. Their violent attack on those who were defenceless brands them as perpetrators of the worst kind of atrocities that one group can commit against another, so in some way they come to epitomize the evil that human beings can do, an evil that must be destroyed. This view is reinforced by the context of the Deuteronomy passage. The command to wipe out Amalek is introduced as taking place 'when the Eternal your God gives you rest from all your enemies round about in the land which the Eternal your God gives you as an inheritance'. That is to say there are at that time no real physical enemies to contend with. Moreover the identical formula

introduces the commandment in Deuteronomy to build a Temple
where they can offer their sacrifices to God (Deut. 12.10f.). The
time will come when Israel is settled in peace on its land, at which
point it will build a place for the presence of God in the world, and
wipe out all memory of evil. This would seem to belong to a
theological picture of the future rather than any real call to arms. It
is the memory of Amalek that is to be blotted out, not Amalek
itself. Nevertheless the existence of such passages gives a licence to
those who wish to demonize a particular group they perceive as
their enemy and we have to acknowledge the problems such
passages in our own sacred scriptures can raise.

As we have seen, the Hebrew Bible contains material that deals
with the *real politik* of its time, with judgments being made on the
political behaviour of Israel and the surrounding nations and
empires. But alongside this can be found prophetic hopes, and some
concrete instructions, about how to bring about a different kind of
ideal future. Each piece has to be examined within its individual
literary context. Moreover we have to make the kind of imaginative
leaps that allow us to enter the biblical world that is being described
for us so as to understand the social and political context in which
Israel operated. But all too often it is difficult to be clear about such
distinctions and, in any event, we always read scripture with our
own expectations and needs in mind.

I would like to conclude with a passage that indicates just how
difficult it is to unscramble the different motivations and values that
may be present in the Hebrew Bible, even where the highest ideals
are being expressed. The passage is the prayer offered by King
Solomon at the opening of the Temple. It is a reflection of his wish
that the Temple become not only the central place of worship for
Israel but also a focus of international acclaim and respect as the
place where Israel's God can be found. However, as Solomon
himself points out:

> Behold the heavens and the heaven of heavens cannot contain
> you, how much less so this house which I have built! (I Kings
> 8.27).

But he goes on to ask God to turn to this place and to answer the
prayers of the king and of Israel. In addition he asks:

> And also every foreigner who is not of Your people Israel who

comes from a distant country for the sake of Your name – for they will hear of Your great name and Your mighty hand and outstretched arm and will come to pray towards this house – may You hear in heaven, the place of Your dwelling, and do according to everything that the foreigner asks of You, so that all the peoples of the earth may know Your name, to fear You like your people Israel and to know that Your name is called upon this house which I have built (I Kings 8.41–43).

But what does Solomon intend with this? Is this the expression of a pious visionary who sees a humanity united under one God? Or of the ruler of a small empire proudly showing off to the world his latest exercise in monumental building? Or is he even a kind of royal entrepreneur trying to encourage the tourist trade with the promise that prayers in Jerusalem are guaranteed an answer? Or perhaps he is a little of all three, because such is the complexity of our human ambitions and actions. Whatever else, it is yet another reminder that the drama of biblical Israel was played out on a world stage and behind all their varying fortunes was the deep commitment to the unity of God and the ultimate unity of humanity. As it was expressed to Abraham at the beginning of the biblical story: through him will all the families of the earth be blessed (Gen. 12.3).

The prophet Zechariah who comes at the end of the biblical period similarly summed up Israel's hope in a phrase that comes at the end of every Jewish service because it expresses that universal vision of a humanity again united under God: 'The Eternal shall be sovereign over all the earth; on that day the Eternal shall be One and known as One' (Zech. 14.9).

5

The Book of Jonah and the Day of Atonement

Somehow I keep finding myself returning to the figure of Jonah. Partly because his book is one of the most accessible in the Hebrew Bible, but also because it remains the most subversive, as I suggested in the first chapter. Such is the quality of the book that it has acquired a very prominent place in later Jewish tradition, and retains its disturbing impact despite Rabbinic attempts to 'tame' the reluctant prophet.

If the Book of Jonah is known to the 'average' Jew, it is because of its central position in the services of *Yom Kippur*, the Day of Atonement, the most solemn fast day in the Jewish Calendar. On this, the tenth day of the Jewish New Year, having considered our sins during the past ten days and attempted to make amends where possible, we fast and attend services all day, in the hope that at the end God will forgive our collective sins and give us a fresh start to the year. It is read in the *minchah*, afternoon, service at the time when people begin to drift back to Synagogue for the close of the Day. One reason for reading it may be inferred from instructions in the Mishnah Ta'anit (2.1) concerning fast days.

What is the order [of service] for fast days [in time of drought]? The ark is taken out to the open space of the city, wood ashes are placed on the ark, on the head of the President and of the Father of the Court. Everyone else puts ashes on his own head. The elder among them speaks to them with words of admonition: 'Brothers, Scripture does not say of the people of Nineveh that God saw their sackcloth and their fasting. But God saw their works that they turned from their evil way (Jonah 3.10). And in the prophets it is said: And rend your heart and not your garments (Joel 2.13).'

On one level this affirms a motif present throughout the Day in the choice of the Haftarah (prophetic) readings. The morning passage from Isaiah emphasizes that mere fasting, 'afflicting your souls', is not the essential feature of the day – rather it is the change in attitude and behaviour that goes with it.

'Why have we fasted if You do not see?
Why afflict ourselves if You pay no heed?'
Because on the day of your fast you put your business first
and force your workers to labour.
Because you only fast for quarrel and strife,
for striking vicious blows.
If that is how you fast this day,
You will not be heard on high.
Is this the fast that I have chosen,
a day for your self-denial?
To bow your head like a bulrush,
to grovel in sackcloth and ashes?
Is this what you call a fast,
a day the Eternal would accept?
Is not *this* the fast I have chosen:
to loosen the fetters of evil,
to untie the straps of the yoke,
to let the oppressed go free,
and whatever the yoke, to break it.
Is it not sharing your food with the hungry
and bringing the homeless into your home;
when you see the naked to clothe them,
never hiding from your own flesh and blood (Isa. 58.3–7).

As usual the translation inevitably misses some of the word plays in the original hebrew text. The verb meaning 'to fast' is *tsum*. In answer to their complaint: 'Why have we fasted if You do not see?', the prophet has God answer: *b'yom tzom'chem timtz'u heifetz* in which the word *timtz'u*, 'you find [your business]' simply reverses the letters of the verb for fasting ('on the day of your *fast* you *stuff*'). And just to underline the way in which their fast is perverse, literally, back-to-front, the next verses finds yet another word which inverts the letters of *tzum*: *l'riv umatzah tatzumu* 'you only fast for quarrel and strife'. (I tried to capture the first pun by translating: on the day of your *fast* you put your business *first*.)

Just as the Isaiah passage challenges the idea of fasting of itself as effective, so the emphasis in Jonah, suggested by the Ta'anit passage, reinforces this view. In this the compilers of the Mishnah have picked up a motif that is actually stressed in the Book of Jonah itself. When the people hear Jonah's words: 'Yet forty days and Nineveh will be overturned', they believed in God and proclaimed a fast and put on sackcloth from the greatest to the least of them (Jonah 3.4, 5). When the news reaches the king he rises from his throne, removes his cloak and covers himself with sackcloth and sits in ashes. In turn he has it proclaimed throughout Nineveh that man and beast, herd and flock, should taste nothing, nor graze nor drink. They should don sackcloth, man and beast, and call aloud to God. Scholars have noted the curious feature that first the people don sackcloth and only subsequently does the king order them to do so. This unnecessary duplication suggests to some that it reflects two different traditions that have been amalgamated. However it is also possible to argue that a wise king takes heed of popular movements and goes along with them. But this threefold repetition of the donning of sackcloth (people, king, decree) may serve another purpose in indicating the conventional response of the people and of those in authority to a threatened disaster. Having established the convention, by repeating it three times, the king's closing words move the whole exercise to a totally new dimension where the ethical act enters and transcends the merely mechanical change of clothing and abstention from food: 'And let each man turn from his evil way and from the violence that is in their hands' (3.8). As Ta'anit indicates, that is the factor that sways God in the decision not to destroy them: 'And God saw their deeds that they turned from their evil way and God repented of the evil which God had threatened to do and did it not (3.10).

Like the passage from Isaiah, the Book of Jonah has a subversive function on this Day. The theological implications of Yom Kippur may be rather hazy to the average Jew at his or her once-a-year attendance in Synagogue, but at least the fast, whether observed or self-consciously ignored, is remembered. And Isaiah and Jonah forcibly remind us that fasting alone is not the essence of the day.

In fact the Book of Jonah has a very uncompromising attitude towards all sorts of pietistic acts which may become substitutes for the real requirements of God. When the sailors are forced to throw Jonah overboard and the sea calms down, in fear of God they make a sacrifice and vow vows. The Midrash (Yalkut Shimeoni ad loc) has them going to Jerusalem and converting to Judaism, which is only spelling out an implication strongly suggested in the story itself. It also indicates that the place to fulfil vows was in a public act at the Temple in Jerusalem, as the Psalms attest (see Ps. 116.14). For the sailors such an act was appropriate – particularly since their prayers have been addressed to the Eternal, Jonah's God. At the end of his 'prayer' in the fish, Jonah uses almost identical language: 'As for me, with the voice of thanksgiving I will make a sacrifice to You; that which I have vowed I will pay' (2.10). Scholars debate the authenticity of the 'psalm' recited by Jonah – was it an original part of the composition of the Book? But since it is present, any interpretation should take it into account. When God has to tell Jonah 'a second time' to go to Nineveh (3.1), it can only be because Jonah's last expressed intention, with all the misplaced piety he can muster, was indeed to go to fulfil his vows and worship God – in Jerusalem! To which God must reply, 'Don't give me your piety, perform My will! Forget Jerusalem and go to Nineveh!'

The theme of the repentance of the Ninevites plays a further essential role in the meaning of the Day. That people can change and that God can forgive, are the hope upon which the dynamic of the Day depends. If the repentance of pagan Nineveh out of fear (only a partial repentance, the Rabbis suggested) could be acceptable to God, how much more so the true repentance of Israel. Yet here too, as the Rabbis recognized, is a potential trap as far as Israel is concerned. One reason for Jonah's flight recorded by Rashi, the great mediaeval Jewish exegete, is precisely his anxiety about Nineveh's repentance: 'If I speak to them and they do repentance, I will make Israel guilty who do not listen to the words of the prophets.'

If pagan Nineveh can repent how much more should Israel, and how much greater the scandal if they do not. This becomes tied to another supposed reason within the Rabbinic tradition for Jonah's reluctance to go there. He knew that Nineveh was to be God's weapon for destroying the Northern kingdom of Israel, and in order to prevent such a catastrophe he was willing to sacrifice his own life by disobeying God and even drowning in the sea. In this he was like Moses and David, both of whom offered their own lives at crucial junctures so as to save Israel. It is hard to avoid the feeling that this reading of Jonah's actions has an apologetic purpose – and it ignores the fact that Jonah could have simply jumped into the sea instead of implicating the sailors, and thus putting their lives at risk, by his act. Furthermore it subverts the universalism of the author whose attitude to Nineveh seems more open. Perhaps Jewish interpretations of Jonah and his relationship with Nineveh can be seen as a measure of the degree of ease or 'at-homeness' the Jewish people feel at any given period of their history in any given place.

However there is another possible reason why Nineveh has significance on this day, through it is less commonly recognized. There are five services on Yom Kippur. If there is a pattern to them, then the first two, the evening service (Kol Nidre) and the morning one, lead towards the central point of the day which takes place in the early afternoon in the 'additional' service. It includes the 'Avodah', the recital and re-enactment of the High Priest's ritual in the Temple on this Sabbath of Sabbaths. In the drama of the High Priest's three confessions (on behalf of himself and his family, of the priesthood and of Israel) and in the choosing of the two goats (one as a sacrifice to God, a sin-offering, and one to be sent into the wilderness symbolically bearing away Israel's sins) lies the mysterious core of this day: the power of confesson to purify, the readiness of God to release people from the accumulated burden of their guilt and purify them from year to year. Though expressed in a symbolic language, which we can only grasp in part, within this service some essential statement is made about the meaning of Israel's existence, and indeed that of the individual Jewish soul. From here the day turns towards its close and in the afternoon service the image of Nineveh suggests the outside world to which we must return from this inner sanctuary. Jonah's ambivalence about Nineveh, his unwillingness to preach there, his anger at their forgiveness, move from the message of the writer to his fellow citizens of whatever period the book was composed, to a challenge to a contemporary Israel, not less uncertain about its relationship with the cities of its exile. For Nineveh is the Rome that destroyed the second Temple, the European countries that spawned the massacres of the Crusaders, the Spanish cities of the Inquisition, the East European centres of pogroms, Berlin of the Third Reich. To all these Ninevehs Jonah is sent, to discover behind 'the violence in their hands' human beings on the verge of repentance awaiting only the word. But Nineveh need not be so dramatic. It is whatever place Jonah does not wish to go because his experience of God is too narrow, his compassion too grudging, his piety too comfortable and convenient. As the day draws to its end, and the 'gates' begin to close (the Neilah service), Jonah forces us to look at this world to which, purified, we must return, with all the myriad tasks and responsibilities that await us there.

And thus it is our own identity and that of the reluctant prophet that indicate yet another dimension of the significance of the Book for this Day.

The reversals of the Book find perhaps their greatest expression in the character of Jonah himself. He is never called a prophet within it, though his role and his presumed identity with the Jonah ben Amitai of II Kings 14.25 imply that he is. As a prophet he expresses the logical extreme of a continuum expressed by the reluctance of other prophets (Moses, Isaiah, Jeremiah) to take up their vocation, and of even attempting to manipulate God's word for their own purposes, as in the case of Balaam (Num. 22–24).[1] Jonah runs away from his task and when confronted finally with the issue, complains bitterly about it, even hurling in God's face the most cherished list of God's attributes of love and mercy (4.2–3).

If we seek a biblical figure to which Jonah is comparable, the most obvious one is the collective character of the children of Israel on their journey through the wilderness – a stiff-necked people grateful at one moment for their rescue from Egypt, and believing in God as a result – and complaining bitterly the next out of discomfort or fear and wishing to return to the security of slavery. Indeed, here we see the most direct evidence that the author may have had such a comparison in mind. When confronted by the Sea of Reeds before them, with Pharaoh's chariots directly behind them, they turn to Moses: 'Is not this the very word which we spoke to you in Egypt saying: Keep away from us and let us serve Egypt, for it is better for us to serve Egypt than that we die in the desert (Ex. 14.12). In an echo of this wording, Jonah addresses God in his long complaint:

> Is not this my very word when I was back in my land – that is why I anticipated and fled to Tarshish, for I knew that You are a God who is gracious and loving, slow to anger and great in mercy, repenting of evil; so now, O Eternal, take my soul from me, for better is my death than my life' (Jonah 4.2–3).

Jonah, who wishes to stay back in his land and not face the

challenges and risks of Nineveh, is equivalent to the Israelites who wish to stay in Egypt and not face the challenges and risks of freedom.

One irony of the story that here emerges is that God's patience (slow to anger) and mercy are more greatly exercised on behalf of the reluctant prophet than they are on evil Nineveh. However at this point I should add one bit of repentance of my own. I used to teach Jonah to a group of therapists in the home of Molly Tuby, a leading analytical psychologist. At one point she stopped me and said that she felt quite attached to Jonah and that perhaps I was being a bit unfair. She liked him because he reminded her so much of some of her neurotic Jewish patients!

Just as the focus of the Book switches between the outer world (Sailors, chapter 1, Nineveh, chapter 3) and the person of Jonah himself (chapters 2,4), so on the Day of Atonement, it is the character of Jonah, the reluctant recipient of God's call, who confronts the Jew in Synagogue, equally confused by the demands and expectations and purpose of his or her complex Jewish identity. Since our natural tendency is to identify with the hero of a story, the author's continual reversal of our expectations, putting Jonah in the wrong, must act upon the reader as well, turning inside out our expectations, assumptions, prejudices and evasions. It is therefore a triumph of the author to end the book with a question mark as God confronts Jonah with the breadth of the divine compassion and the limits of Jonah's understanding, and awaits an answer. The question is thus addressed to the reader no less than to Jonah, with no guarantee what the reply will be, for that is God's risk at the heart of the relationship with human beings in the biblical reading of history. Having eaten the fruit of the tree of knowledge of good and evil we are free to choose for or against God. And God must cajole, threaten, challenge, command, tempt and even beg, in the hope of our loving return.

In the Book, Jonah gives no answer, and that is right within the drama of the Book itself, but religious traditions have felt the need of some reassuring affirmation at the end.

Already in the Rabbinic Midrash a response is found for Jonah. To God's question, a repentant and weeping Jonah falls on his face and says: Guide Your world with the attribute of mercy, as it says: 'To the Eternal our God belong compassion and forgiveness' (Dan. 9.9). In much the same way the Rabbis provided a more satisfactory prayer for Jonah to recite in the belly of the fish than his 'psalm' with its lack of any statement of repentance.

> God of the worlds: whither can I go from Your spirit, and whither can I flee from Your presence? If I rise up to heaven ... (Ps. 139.7, 8) You are Sovereign over all the kingdoms and master of all the princes of the world; Your throne is the heaven of heavens and the earth is Your footstool; Your kingdom is on high and your rule in the depths. The deeds of all people are revealed before You and the secret things of every person are perceived by You; You search out the way of all people, and test the steps of all living beings; You know the secrets of the emotions (lit. kidneys) and understand the hidden thoughts of the heart; all mysteries are revealed to You, nothing is hidden from the throne of Your glory and nothing is concealed from Your eyes; every secret You order and every word You consider; in every place You are there; Your eyes seek out the bad and the good. May it please You to answer me from the belly of Sheol [the underworld] and save me from the deep; let my cry come to Your ears and fulfil my request. For You dwell afar off and hear from close by. You are called the One who raises up and brings down – please raise me up. You are called the One who slays and gives life – I have reached death, give me life (Yalkut Shimoni, Jonah).

It is the scandal of Jonah's stubbornness that evokes these responses, this desire for reassurance that the prophet will obey. Braver is the Midrash which, though critical of Jonah, recognizes a legitimate tension between the respect due to human beings and that due to God.

> There were three prophets: one defended both the honour of the father (God) and the honour of the son (Israel); one defended the honour of the father rather than the honour of the son; and one defended the honour of the son rather than the honour of the father. Jeremiah defended both the honour of the father and the honour of the son, as it is written (Lam. 3.42 – accredited in Jewish tradition to Jeremiah): 'We have transgressed and rebelled; You have not pardoned ...' Elijah defended the honour of the father rather than the honour of the son, as it is written (I Kings 19.14): 'I have been zealous for the Eternal, God of hosts; for the children of Israel have forsaken Your covenant, thrown

down Your altars and slain Your prophets with the sword'
. . . Jonah defended the honour of the son rather than the
honour of the father, as it says (Jonah 3.1): 'The word of the
Eternal came to Jonah a second time . . .' (Mechilta, Bo).

Yet putting Jonah into the framework of Yom Kippur must subtly
change the nature of the final question and its missing answer. For at
stake on this day is the future of all Israel, the collective nation
stands this day in judgment, personified by the prophet, but not
dependent on one person's choice. When Israel confronts God on
this day, they are conscious of the merits of the fathers, Abraham,
Isaac and Jacob, that support them, the promises of the covenant to
the whole people, and the millennial task that has led them to act as
a faithful 'servant of the Eternal' in every place and every age, at
home and in exile, in suffering and joy. So Jonah, for all the subtlety
and challenge of the Book, is not given the final word. For it is not
the ego of a single individual that determines Israel's fate on this
day, but the mercy of God – which is, after all, the lesson a reluctant
Jonah must also learn. So to God's final question to Jonah comes an
answering prayer in the second reading from the prophets that
accompanies Jonah, taken from the Book of Micah.

Who is a God like You that pardons the iniquity
and passes over the rebellion
of the remnant of God's heritage;
Who does not hold anger forever
but desires mercy;
Who will again have compassion on us;
Who will subdue our iniquities
and You will cast into the depth of the seas all their sins.
You will show faithfulness to Jacob
mercy to Abraham
as You swore to our ancestors
from the days of old (Micah 7.18–20).

Jonah ends with a question; the Day of Atonement ends with a
great affirmation. Yet, in the words of my teacher Rav Shmuel
Sperber:

Religion provides answers without removing the question . . . a
question can contain a great religious truth.

It is the Jonah whose response we can never guarantee who affirms our freedom, yet teases us into an uncomfortable recognition of our own self-deception. That is why in the end he is such an admirable, subversive companion on the Day of Atonement as between Tarshish and Nineveh we sail our stormy sea, awaiting our private encounter with the maw of the great fish.

6

The Biblical Roots of
Jewish Identity

*This chapter serves as a bridge between the two parts of this book. It
began life as a paper to a Jewish audience about the nature of Jewish
identity today and how far it was rooted in the Hebrew Bible. When I
was invited to deliver the ninth annual J S O T (Journal for the Study
of the Old Testament) lecture at the University of Sheffield in 1992, it
seemed useful to put that original paper into the wider context of the
subjectivity of our study of the Bible. We approach the Hebrew Bible
(or, for that matter, the Old Testament) out of our own context, with
our own presuppositions, most of which we hardly recognize. So my
original paper was offered as an example of a subjective reading, to a
Jewish audience about a Jewish concern, and this new audience was
invited to eavesdrop and thus consider the assumptions that lay
behind their own reading. The article was subsequently published
and I reproduce it here with a few amendments to illustrate how the
internal 'self-questioning' of the Hebrew Bible has to continue into
the worlds of those who study it and use it, whether within their own
religious tradition or in the supposedly objective world of academic
scholarship. We make the Bible in our own image.*

Reading the Hebrew Bible is always a subjective exercise, whatever
the particular discipline we use. In the past, those who studied the
Bible within their own faith community, brought to it the concerns
of that community, with a greater or lesser awareness of other
audiences that might be interested in what they found – and those
were also likely to be of a religious persuasion. The emergence of
'modern Bible scholarship' in the wake of the Enlightenment broke
that old religious monopoly, or rather was itself a part of the
struggle for emancipation from what were perceived as religious
constraints upon the 'true' understanding of the text. The 'scientific'

study of the Bible itself worked within certain sets of assumptions which brought considerable gains, but also certain limitations. For example, by reacting against what was perceived as a narrow or partisan religious exegesis, it often failed to acknowledge the spiritual perspective of the text. Conversely, the biblically based religions that found themselves so much under threat from the forces unleashed by the Enlightenment, felt the need to defend themselves through a new fundamentalism against what they perceived as an onslaught on their central religious texts.

The issue of the religious versus the secular reading of scripture remains very present in a variety of ways still today, though there have also been surprising resolutions. The paradoxes of the current situation were dramatized for me at one of the annual Jewish-Christian Bible conferences that I organize in Germany. For years the largely Christian audience had been satisfied with learning about Jewish exegesis of the particular texts – and in Germany there are obvious historical as well as spiritual reasons for this. But in time a reaction began to set in and the demand came for an 'authentic' Christian exegesis of the texts we were studying. But what did they mean by authentic Christian exegesis today? The Jewish teachers could draw on midrash, the Rabbinic exegesis that covers a period from the second century BCE till the ninth century CE, and also on the great tradition of mediaeval Jewish scholarship with figures like Rashi, Ibn Ezra, Radak, Nahmanides, Sforno and Shadal (Shmuel David Luzzatto) carrying us into the late nineteenth century.[1] We could also draw in scholars like Martin Buber and Franz Rosenzweig, Abraham Joshua Heschel and Andre Neher, Umberto Cassuto, Benno Jacob and, in her own unique way, Nehama Leibowitz,[2] who have helped create bridges between traditional Jewish exegesis and the newer literary analysis of our own time. But for the Christians, the mediaeval period seemed relatively unknown territory and not particularly relevant because too much of the exegetical tradition was concerned with typology and not too directly connected with an analysis of the text in its actual context.[3] Continuity with the past seemed to be broken. So what was the modern Christian exegesis they wanted? The answer they gave was a proper theological interpretation of the Yahwist, Elohist, Deuteronomist and Priestly sources.

Now it is not for me to define in what way such an exercise would or would not be authentically 'Christian', but it was fascinating to see how far scientific postulates about the possible sources of certain texts had acquired an existence of their own and even a specific religious identity.

The point I wish to make is simply that it is important that at some level we seek to acknowledge the particular agenda that we bring to our studies or at least recognize some of the presuppositions that colour both the questions that we ask of the text and the answers that we find. The problem is how do we set about uncovering our own agenda and the limits it imposes on our exegesis?

One possible solution is to set up a kind of dialogue process whereby we examine with others the presuppositions we each bring to the text. So this chapter is an attempt to describe some of the questions that I bring to the Hebrew Bible from the Jewish world in which I operate as a scholar and a Rabbi. I hope that such an approach will create responses that will help us see more clearly the assumptions that underlie them.

This chapter began life as an address to a Jewish audience. It was an attempt to explore the complexity of Jewish identity today, but using the Hebrew Bible and the way it has been understood in Jewish tradition as a focal point. In today's fragmented Jewish world, the issue of 'identity' seems to be one of major concern. Abraham's descendants have been both a people and a religious community, these two elements being inextricably intertwined. But since the Enlightenment and Emancipation major divisions have appeared both between these two components of Jewish identity and within them. As the Hebrew Bible has been the source to which Jews have always turned when seeking solutions to their contemporary problems, it seemed reasonable to do so again with this issue. In some ways the problem of identity, whether expressed in religious or national or other terms, is a common one for Western people, so I would hope that this somewhat particularistic exercise will have wider echoes.

The Hebrew Bible and Judaism

At first glance the subject 'The Biblical Roots of Jewish Identity' may seem anachronistic. Jews tend to take for granted that our origins are described in the Hebrew Bible, and that there is a direct continuity between the characters it describes, the Jewish people that emerge from its pages, and our own existence today. Of course we recognize that since the close of the Biblical canon there have been some two thousand years of Jewish diaspora history, during which time we have interacted with almost all the nations and races on the earth and that it would be very difficult to detect many drops of authentic Abrahamic blood inside us. But nevertheless, physically, culturally, spiritually we trace our origins to the Bible in an almost automatic, unquestioning way.

However there are a number of issues that have to be raised. Firstly, the Hebrew Bible is only our Bible because at a certain point in time, the Rabbis, the creators of the Rabbinic Judaism that has shaped our identity, said that it was. It was they who determined what it should contain and, more importantly, how it should be used, valued and interpreted. Moreover, they also asserted that alongside the written Torah given to Moses at Sinai, was a tradition of interpretation, the Oral Torah, that alone helped us understand what the written Torah meant. In this sense it is Judaism that has determined what the Bible is, rather than the Bible determining what Judaism, and hence Jewish identity, is.

This is a view expressed by one of the foremost, if most radical, Orthodox Jewish thinkers today, the late Professor Yeshayahu Leibowitz. He died in his nineties, a renowned scholar of the history of medicine and of Judaism, an authority on Maimonides and, as a lifelong Zionist, a strong critic of trends in Israel, particularly with regard to the treatment of its Arab population. But all his work is based on his view of *halachah*, Jewish law, as representing the supreme value in Judaism. He writes:

> Judaism is not founded on the Bible; the Bible is founded upon Judaism! The meaning of the twenty-four Books derives from the value and the place which Judaism assigned them. Why should we accept these twenty-four Books as the supreme value and not simply as old literature but for the decision of the *halachah*, that they are sacred books? *halachah*, called in Jewish tradition the Oral Law, decided what were the Holy Scriptures of Judaism. The Written Law derives its dignity and its value from the decisions of the Oral Law.[4]

Leibowitz uses this argument to assert that *halachah* in its narrowest possible sense is the only thing that defines Judaism, which incidentally allows him to disenfranchise Reform and Conservative Judaism and secular Jews of any sort. But the point he makes, that it is a particular group of a particular community at a particular time that defined what the Hebrew Bible was for us, is an argument that has consequences for his own Orthodox position. For the issue between, for example Orthodox and Reform Jews, ceases to be about the truth of divine revelation, but about timebound human interpretations and the authority of those who interpret.

In her book *Standing Again at Sinai: Judaism from a Feminist Perspective*, Judith Plaskow makes the identical point in arguing that it was a masculine community within an existing patriarchal society that created Judaism, and defined the identity and place of women within it. She writes:

> Just as Jews of the past experienced God and interpreted their experiences in communal contexts that shaped what they saw and heard, so we also read their words and experiences of God in communities – communities in continuity with, but different from, theirs. It is the contemporary feminist community that has taught me to value and attend to women's experience. It is this community that has taught me that Jewish sources have been partial and oppressive, occasionally ugly and simply wrong . . .
>
> To locate authority in particular communities of interpreters is admittedly to make a circular appeal. Yet it is also to acknowledge what has always been the case: that in deciding what is authoritative in sacred texts, deciding communities take authority to themselves. When the rabbis said that rabbinic modes of interpretation were given at Sinai, they were claiming authority for their own community – just as other groups had before them, just as feminists do today.[5]

We could probably add to her categories of groups within the Jewish world today that interpret and claim authority for their interpretation, Liberal, Reform, Conservative, Reconstructionist, modern Orthodox and Hasidic Jews, as well as Zionist, Humanist and Secularist Jews. In short, there are as many Judaisms today as there are Jewish groups that claim authority for their perception and have those who support them. And each of these groups will have a different perspective upon the authority, authenticity and significance of the Hebrew Bible in determining at least some aspect of their Jewish identity. For some Zionists it takes on a priority in underpinning their claim to the land of Israel, and indeed it has acquired a new life today in the ongoing debate within Israel about the extent of the biblical territory and the way in which Arab inhabitants should be treated. For Reform Jews, at least of an earlier period in the United States, it offered, through the writings of the Prophets, a justification for their strong social conscience and activism and universalism. For others it is the tradition of Rabbinical interpretation that has determined not only what parts of the Bible still speak, but how they speak and how they are to be developed or modified to fit particular needs. For feminists, it is the gaps that have to be filled, the absent women's voices that have to be sought, so that a fairer and more rounded picture of Jewish identity and existence is to be discovered.

In short we are in a period of relativity as regards every aspect of Jewish tradition, and in a way, the louder the cries by any party about their own authenticity, the greater the denial of the complexity of today's Jewish world and the more partial their own position. There is no single Jewish identity, but Jewish identities of considereble variety. So our exploration of the biblical roots of these identities can only be partial, offering approaches that may be explored further.

Hebrews, Jews or just plain human beings?

There is a second problem that stands in the way of our direct identification with the biblical materials. It may seem to be only a technicality, but it is crystallized in a remark I overheard from an actor taking part in the biblical epic, *King David*, on which I was the technical adviser.[6] He was discussing with the other actors how to play their parts in the film. Should they put on a Jewish accent or not? No, said the actor, you can play them like normal people because they weren't Jews yet!

What he meant is that biblical Israel was a people with a national identity and for a large part of their existence had their own sovereign state, though for a while it existed as two states side-by-side. It was the southern kingdom Judah that gave us the name Judaean, and hence ultimately the word 'Jew'. In a technical sense, before the Kingdom of Judah came into existence 'Jews' were still 'the children of Israel', the descendants of the patriarch Jacob who was also called Israel, and officially not Judaeans, and certainly not Jews. But on another level, and as the actor so clearly understood it, it was the experience of exile, captivity and two thousand years of wandering that created the 'Jew' of the popular stereotype, the one with the Jewish accent. Two thousand years of living as a minority people under the power structures of other societies and religions helped form many of the characteristics seen as 'Jewish'.

That is one of the reasons that the Bible was such an important resource for those building the State of Israel, especially David Ben Gurion. It promised a way of stepping outside of Diaspora Jewish history with its tragedy and conditioning, its ghetto mentality and paranoia, its need to appease and give way to others, to return to the days of independence in thought and action, to a free people wedded to the soil of their own land. It also meant a radical break with the restrictive traditional religion of the ghetto which seemed to foster a paralysis of action and thought while waiting for God to act on our behalf.

On that negative reading there is no connection between contemporary Jewish identity, at least in the Diaspora, and the heroic figures and images of our biblical past. Of course it is not as simple as that. Diaspora Jewry has its own kind of heroism and biblical characters can be weak in many ways. Moreover the biblical record is always read in a selective way to justify whatever limited goals any particular group may have. Even those Jews who try to return to some assumed 'original meaning' of the biblical record do so with a bias, if only because of the conscious attempt to read them afresh and suppress the layers of Rabbinic imagination that overlay them. This desire for going back to the origins helps explain the deep Israeli interest in archaeology. It is not only that it reinforces a sense of Jewish belonging to that particular piece of territory when things relating to that past are excavated. It is also a way of claiming an authentic pre-rabbinic way of understanding what was going on, when we were still Hebrews in the land of Canaan. An orthodox Rabbinic friend of mine in Jerusalem once pointed out how reverently the Israelis have treated the Isaiah scroll from the Dead Sea. After all the same text exists in the printed bibles they get from school and the army. But nevertheless they handle it with a sort of reverence that is astonishing for allegedly secular people. It can be no accident, he felt, that the place it is housed in the Israel Museum is called 'The shrine of the scroll'. 'If an archaeologist ever dug up God,' he suggested, 'the whole country would become believers!'

Nevertheless for two thousand years Jews have read these stories, interpreted them, interpreted the interpretations, and tried to understand them at the deepest possible level as our stories about our family and about us. But whether we seek in the Bible stories characters from Jewish history, or the role models of our Rabbinic period, in what sense are they Jewish?

The patriarchs display typical human characteristics and patterns of behaviour, but also evoke very specific echoes in a Jewish consciousness as we read their stories and adventures. Perhaps such an effect is really the result of a circular reasoning on our part – the biblical narratives shaped Jewish interpretation which in turn shaped Jewish consciousness which now feeds back into our understanding of these characters. Alternatively we might evoke the 'archetypes' of C.G.Jung and suggest that there is indeed imprinted into our existence as a people certain characteristics of thought and behaviour which are reflected in the biblical characters, and which emerge still today, if only in our dreams and in the things we say on the psychoanalyst's couch. I suppose we choose whichever theory we find most congenial. The patriarchs may indeed reflect some essential Jewish characteristics re-emerging in different variations in each generation. But they may equally be a sort of screen on to which we project our contemporary *human* experience, coloured by the particular circumstances of our own Jewish life. If the latter they would be no more and no less Jewish than they would be Christian or would belong to the particular faith or non-faith of any serious reader. Determining the 'Jewishness' of the patriarchs is as difficult as determining our own Jewishness today! Let us look at some biblical characters and see how this problem works itself out.

Abraham the patriarch, who set out at the age of seventy to found a religion, fits well with a traditional Jewish value system that venerates the wisdom and learning of the aged – though such values have been eroded today in the youth culture in which we live. Abraham's domestic troubles, in fact those of all the patriarchs, seem very familiar, though as human realities rather than as specifically Jewish. But what are we to make of the *Akedah*, the binding of Isaac, when Abraham almost sacrifices his son for the sake of his God? One can believe that of a Victorian Abraham perhaps, but it is not very comfortable in our contemporary social context nor is it the sort of behaviour that Jews actually get up to! As we shall see, the Rabbis also had to find ways of dealing with this extraordinary behaviour.

In terms of the biblical narratives themselves, Isaac appears to be the most colourless of the patriarchs. He seems like the withdrawn or repressed son of a famous father, overwhelmed by him and his expectations, and perhaps traumatized by the events of the *Akedah*. Nevertheless he maintains the direction and the work of Abraham in his stubborn, solemn way, literally redigging and protecting the wells his father established in the promised land, ensuring the continuity of that link.

With Jacob we have a much more familiar Jewish stereotype in both positive and negative ways – the complex manipulator of events and people who nevertheless is forced to struggle with himself and accept his religious task. But in this sense he also conforms to the character of the 'trickster' who can be found in many other cultures as well.

Joseph likewise fits a famework familiar in Jewish life, the spoiled gifted child who becomes the victim of his brothers' jealousy, but again this is also a universal problem. However in his rise to power in a foreign environment, becoming Pharaoh's Vizier, he does seem to be the prototype of all those Jewish advisers and counsellors to monarchs and potentates who have continually reappeared throughout Jewish history, especially those who also accepted responsibility for the welfare of the Jewish community. But again, in what sense are these particularly Jewish figures or Jewish characteristics of behaviour?

And so the argument can go backwards and forwards with each of the major characters – their humanity may also reflect a Jewish humanity, but in no way exclusively so. Why should Jews be able to claim them more than any other people might who also turn to the Bible for inspiration or understanding of the religious quest.

What of biblical events? Here we seem to be on slightly safer ground. For major aspects of the Jewish myth, our Jewish self-understanding, derive from certain key events in the biblical story. At the Passover meal every year, perhaps the one event in Jewish life that actually still affects major parts of Jewish society, each of us is asked to consider ourselves as if we came out from Egypt, experienced the journey from slavery to freedom. In similar ways Rabbinic exegesis has each of us standing at Sinai and experiencing revelation. Each of us has journeyed in a wilderness towards a promised land that always seems to evade us, dwelling in fragile shelters on the way. As Tisha B'Av reminds us, the fast of the ninth day of the month of Av which commemorates the destruction of both Temples, we have also lived in such a land and seen it torn away from us and felt the pain of exile.

These archetypal events of Jewish self-understanding that accompany our liturgical year and childhood memories also play their part in shaping our identity and character. Though each element may not be a uniquely Jewish experience, the combination must reflect and in turn create something that is special to us alone. Provided only that Jews are still operating somewhere within these parameters of traditional Jewish experience.

The need for stories

Having suggested that Jews see the Bible through the particular filter of two thousand years of Rabbinic tradition and interpretation, perhaps we should now examine something of that effect in the way it has shaped Jewish self-understanding and identity. The various Rabbinic midrashim around the figures of the Patriarchs and other biblical heroes help illustrate the process. The Rabbis often remade them in their own image – sometimes as a way of establishing their own authority and credentials by claiming a venerable ancestry. Thus the military figures like King David and his general Joab become transformed by the Rabbis from warriors with the sword to heroes of piety and learning!

When David first appears he is described as *admoni im y'fey eynaim*, 'ruddy with beautiful eyes' (I Sam. 16.12). The midrash has the prophet Samuel worried because David was 'ruddy'. He said: 'Surely this one will shed blood like Esau, who was also called 'ruddy' (Gen. 25.25)'. But God said to him, 'However "he has beautiful eyes". Esau killed at will, while this one will live by justice and only kill by the consent of the Sanhedrin, the Rabbinic court, who are the eyes of Israel' (Midrash Shmuel 19.6; Genesis Rabba 66.8).

According to the midrash Pesikta Rabbati (11.3) Joab the general was really a sage, the head of the Sanhedrin (the supreme court of justice), great in Torah study and only incidentally a military warrior. Indeed the Talmud, in Tractate Sanhedrin 49a, goes so far as to suggest that Joab was of such a refined, scholarly disposition that 'were it not for David, Joab would never have waged war;

conversely, were it not for Joab, David would never have studied Torah!'

For the Rabbis David became not only a Torah scholar, but inspired others to do the same. In Pesikta Rabbati (17.3) we find a comment on the verse in Psalm 119.62, 'At midnight I will rise to give thanks to You because of Your judgments, Your mercy.' 'What did David do? He would take a psaltery and a harp, put them at the head of his couch, and rising at midnight would play upon them. At this the studious people, hearing the sound of David playing, would say, "If David, king of Israel, can study Torah at midnight, so much the more so should we!" And so all Israel studied Torah.'

The Rabbis were preachers and teachers, addressing the particular needs of their contemporaries, and using the biblical stories as ways of interpreting events and advising on how to act. In difficult times, under Roman persecution, they would even use a kind of code to allow themselves to speak about the Romans without getting into trouble with the authorities. Thus Esau, also known in the Bible as Edom, becomes a symbol for Rome. Hence all the stories about the struggles between Jacob and Esau could be interpreted to refer to current events, which helps ex lain why the Rabbis spent so much time defaming Esau and justifying Jacob. They utilized a principle that works well both as an exegetical tool in evaluating some of the stories in Genesis and Exodus and as a homiletic device: *ma'aseh avot siman l'vanim*, 'the actions of the fathers (the patriarchs) are signs for the children' (Sotah 34a).[7] That is to say the journeys and adventures of the patriarchs are re-enacted by their descendants. In fact this is an interesting observation when we examine the patriarchal narratives, particularly those relating to exile from the land and their visits to Egypt, and compare them to the Exodus narratives. But this principle can also be used by the Rabbis to provide the Jewish people with models of behaviour for their own situations. For example, when Jacob was about to confront Esau after his long exile, being still fearful of his brother's reaction, he sent a number of gifts ahead of himself as a sort of bribe. The Rabbis examining Jacob's behaviour recognized in it three strategies to be pursued when faced with similar threats of aggression against the Jewish people. First try to appease with a gift; then pray to God to intervene and save; but in case all else fails, prepare to fight.

Similarly Abraham becomes in Rabbinic eyes the ideal of hospitality and friendliness. His tent was open to the four directions and he would go out of his way to bring wayfarers in. After feeding them, when they thanked him, he would tell them not to thank him but the God who had provided the food. In this way he drew them into accepting Israel's God. While Abraham converted the men in this way, Sarah converted the women. Which presumably reflects a missionizing tendency in Rabbinic Judaism that was later suppressed.

I mentioned before the problems the Rabbis had with the *Akedah*, the story of the binding of Isaac, and there are many midrashim addressing the problem of how Abraham could agree to God's request and exploring the inner debate that he went through during the three day journey to the place of sacrifice. But what is significant is that in this particular case they do *not* apply the formula given above. This event in Abraham's life never becomes a model for later behaviour. Instead it is suggested that the Jewish people continues to exist because of the merit of Abraham's faithful act so that there is no need for us ourselves to repeat such a thing. In a sense they domesticated Abraham, remaking him in their own image and value system.

But it is precisely here that a point of contact is made with us today. For the stories of the patriarchs, in their biblical and Rabbinic form, are still available as models of behaviour or as evocative ways of reflecting on our own situations – domestic and national. The way the story is told reflects back to us as a mirror our own reality and suggests ways of coping with it. The problem today in society at large is that we tend to relegate story-telling of this sort to the nursery, and in Jewish terms we have lost much of the direct line of contact we once had with this rich source of Rabbinic legend and lore.

But the need for such enrichment of our imagination still exists, except that we experience it in a secular form. In place of Abraham and Sarah, Isaac and Rebeccah, today's real heroes and heroines, our role models, no longer walk the streets of Jerusalem or Beersheba, but inhabit the ranchhouses of Dallas and the suburbs of Australia. The soaps, which are watched with the attention, devotion and love that no contemporary religious stories can command, contain the images and values that actually shape our sense of reality. Whatever need such materials fill, was once met in part by the religious legends of the great spiritual traditions. Only then, it was the familiarity of the stories, their predictability, and their consistency and certainties, that made them part of our unified religious, cultural and social life. In a traditional society, these heroes and their stories had their place within the family circle, while at the same time being open to the most sophisticated interpretation and re-interpretation, because they addressed the needs of the outer world.

Today in our larger more complex society the same need for reassurance and pattern in our life would seem to be there; it is just that we prefer the illusion of change and surprise in our weekly episode, even if the underlying plots and characterizations are essentially the same. Whether one form of storytelling and self-mirroring is more profound than the other hardly matters. We are experiencing a new universalism whereby the same television series has, over the long term, the same impact on formerly different cultures and civilizations. The same values are emulated and assimilated unconsciously all over the world. Against such persuasive power the old traditional tales somehow lack glamour or relevance. And if they are transferred on to the small screen, the very demands of that medium convert them into the same banal commonplaces as the others. Because the effectiveness of the traditional stories lies in our personal engagement with them, with their resonances within us, as much as it does with the plot line. Hearing the stories helped shape our sense of being in the world and demanded our participation in the experience. Moreover they were meant for adults to make them more adult and not just for children. Instead the soaps render us passive. They infantilize us by doing it all for us and converting everything into the same undifferentiated fare. Since we only learn our traditional stories today as children we also remain spiritual infants, never probing them with our adult minds. In this sense, we have perhaps never been further away from the Bible in seeking to shape our Jewish or any other identity.

Re-imagining the Bible

So far I have remained within a recognizable Jewish exegetical tradition. But it may be helpful for our broader purpose of exploring the limits of contemporary Jewish exegesis to go considerably further afield. Precisely because the edges of Jewish identity and the nature of Jewish experience are so blurred today it is important to test out how far they can be stretched and still remain both recognizably Jewish and true in some sense to the Hebrew Bible. The following are therefore some fairly random examples from the borderlines.

The Bible still seems to affect Jews in unexpected ways, even in their marginal Judaism and their commitment to secular, humanist values. Sigmund Freud in his last book, written when he was over eighty, returned to the subject of religion with a study of Moses, *Moses and Monotheism.*[8] He reversed the biblical story, seeing Moses as an Egyptian who taught monotheism to the Hebrews and was killed by them when they rebelled against him. This event was concealed in the biblical account but nevertheless it had given rise to a self-perpetuating guilt feeling in the Jewish people. One of Freud's biographers[9] has suggested that Freud was here reflecting his own ambiguity about his relationship with Judaism – that he too felt himself to be really an Egyptian prince mistakenly raised within a Jewish family. But whatever one makes of Freud's interpretation, it is clear that the figure of Moses strongly affected him and in his way he was also creating a contemporary midrash on the biblical narratives. (We should also note that in the wake of Freud psychoanalytic and psychotherapeutic insights have frequently been applied to biblical materials.)[10]

Novels and plays using the figure of King David seem to have multiplied in recent years. The South African novelist Dan Jacobson gave a highly cynical account of the Biblical narrative surrounding David's disastrous family life in his short novel *The Rape of Tamar.*[11] In a similar vein, the German Jewish novelist Stefan Heym created a devastating attack on the way history was constantly being re-written in Eastern Europe under the communist regimes in his novel *The King David Report.*[12] In order to consolidate his kingdom, Solomon orders a scribe to write the official authentic report on the rise of King David and his appointment of Solomon as his successor. Unfortunately the scribe knows too much of the truth about what went on, and has access to David's ex-wives, so he sneaks into the surface praise of the great king a range of incidents and materials that hint at the feet of clay. Even though the scholarship on which Heym's book is based is now somewhat dated, it is brilliantly successful because he knows how to read the biblical text and recognize the different perceptions of the

King that it actually contains. And he is too good a novelist to let his polemic destroy his art. Here is also a classic example of a biblical text fulfilling a subversive purpose in a later generation.[13]

A quite different exercise has taken place this century with the biblical Book of Jeremiah. The prophet saw the rise of the Babylonian empire as an act of God, and prophesied that unless the people of Judah and Jerusalem turned back from their internal violence and sin, they would be destroyed. For this view he was persecuted, imprisoned and threatened with death. After the destruction of Jerusalem he became the great comforter of the people. The writer Stefan Zweig took him as the central character in his verse drama *Jeremiah*.[14] Written during the First World War it was performed in Zurich before the war was over, and stands as a great pacifist statement. In his autobiography Zweig writes about the play:

> I had not intended to write a 'pacifist' play, or to set in words and verses the truth that peace was better than war, but to portray the man who in time of enthusiasm is despised as a weakling, the timid one, but in the hour of defeat proves himself to be the only one able to endure it.[15]

In a different way the novelist Franz Werfel also wrote about the prophet seeing in him the ecstatic visionary standing out against the crowd. His novel about Jeremiah, *Hearken to the Voice*,[16] begins and ends with the experience of a diaspora Jew on a visit to Palestine and brings in the theme of a future restoration.

Perhaps the most significant explorer of biblical materials is Franz Kafka who in a few terse parables explored themes like the tower of Babel, the character of Abraham and, perhaps most importantly the Torah, understood as 'The Law'.

He tells a parable in his novel *The Trial*[17] about the man from the country who wishes to visit the Law and is not admitted by the gatekeeper. The keeper warns the man that even if he gets past him, there is a second gatekeeper beyond him who is stronger and fiercer than himself and a whole succession of gatekeepers beyond even that. The man from the country is puzzled because he had thought that the Law was available to everybody. So he waits beside the gatekeeper for years hoping to be allowed in. In the end, when he is old and dying, he asks the keeper why in all these years no one else has come to be admitted. The keeper leans down to him and explains that this gate was only for him and he is now closing it.

It would appear that Kafka had in mind a Rabbinic midrash when creating this parable. The midrash (Midrash Haggadol to Exodus 24.18) tells that when Moses went up to the top of Mount Sinai to obtain the Torah, he stepped on to a cloud and walked as if on solid ground. Then an angel challenged him and asked where he was going. 'To get the Torah,' replied Moses. 'You cannot,' said the angel, 'for I am here to stop you. And if you get past me there is another angel who is bigger and fiercer than I am, and beyond him one so fierce that even I am scared of him.' But instead of giving up at that point, Moses simply pushes the angel aside and strides on. When he meets the second angel, which is indeed more fearsome than the first, Moses too is frightened but God intervenes and orders this second angel to conduct him past the others so as to get the Torah.

Both passages are mysterious, but it has always seemed to me that Kafka is writing in part about his own estrangement from the Torah, the Law. Our alienation from the tradition is so great that we never get past the first hurdle and merely wait hopefully by the gatekeeper, even bribing him if necessary, rather than going on to claim our heritage. There may be many other ways of interpreting, but here, with Kafka, we have precisely that retelling and reinterpretation of the Bible, this time as mediated through the Rabbinic tradition, that challenges us and forces us to look afresh, and in an adult way, at the teachings themselves.

Naming just these few authors and works is only to scratch the surface. In all these cases the starting point within the Bible is clear, but a whole variety of biblical themes, like the struggle between Cain and Abel, the Exodus from Egypt, the suffering of Job and a myriad others, serve as the basis for countless writings. Though in our fragmented culture today the authors may only be partly aware of this original influence.[18]

But in what way, if at all, are the interpretations of modern Jewish writers like the above 'Jewish interpretations', particularly when they themselves may make no claim to work within any recognizable Jewish mode, or even identify themselves as particularly Jewish? On one level they may simply be taken as universalistic works – with themes we have mentioned like 'pacifism', 'the falsification of history', 'the alienation of modern people'. If so, the biblical characters or stories or background are merely convenient pegs for the writer. But it may also be argued that at this stage in the twentieth century the classical Jewish modes of expression have fallen away or become dissipated, except for those who operate within formal religious structures. Perhaps in this chaos, whatever Jews say, write or do, however marginal they may be, is helping to determine a new Judaism that will eventually emerge.

Whenever Jews moved from one culture to another there was a process of change, assimilation and redefining over a period of generations. Perhaps these writers, some of whom do identify themselves as Jewish, will prove to be part of a new synthesis between Jewish tradition and the contemporary world, and their writings will prove to be tentative explorations of what a new Jewish identity and a new Jewish exegesis might be. As always in the middle of such a process we are more conscious of what has been lost than of what, if anything, has been gained. But we should remember that if we only had the Hebrew Bible before us, it would have been very difficult if not impossible to have predicted that two religions as different as Rabbinic Judaism and Christianity could have emerged from it, each claiming an authentic line of continuity. It took centuries before the Talmud became a sort of new 'scripture' to set alongside the old one, and indeed the Zohar similarly became a third Jewish 'scripture' for the growth of Jewish mystical tradition. A future Judaism may well have yet another 'scripture' to treasure alongside the others, one in which Kafka at least may well find his place. Perhaps in thousands of years time, on some distant planet, a Jewish community, hardly recognizable as even human, will pore over copies of *The Trial* with the same love and dedication that is devoted today to the Talmud. The Science Fiction writer Harlan Ellison[19] has already written a story about a future where a blue-skinned, multi-eyed, eleven-armed, yiddish-speaking Jew on the planet Theta 996–VI studies the stories of Abraham in a yeshiva, and Sci-Fi writers may well be today's prophets!

New images of the Jew

If the above material has been somewhat speculative, I would like to go even further afield, perhaps to the point of absurdity, just to indicate the breadth of the problem. How far can one trace uniquely biblical or Jewish contributions to contemporary Western culture?

let me note one minor but intriguing example in the form of a character in a comic strip that was the creation of two young American Jews, Joe Shuster and Jerry Siegel.

When mild-mannered Clark Kent, the reporter of the *Daily Planet*, takes off his suit he becomes Superman, the first and perhaps the greatest of the superheroes. What is the biblical or Jewish element in this character? It is certainly arguable that he reflects the fantasies of the powerless ghetto Jew, the product of two thousand years of exile. Beneath the seemingly cowed and apologetic exterior lies his real strength that he has had to suppress throughout the centuries. Remember that the first Superman cartoon strip appeared in 1938 and what the Jewish world was experiencing at that time! Certainly this Hercules-type figure is not too far from the projection on to the first generation of Israeli sabras by their parents, the early immigrations to Israel. But this dual identity has earlier roots. A Clark Kent who is really Superman is also a variation on the theme of the two names of Jacob/Israel which change back and forth within the Bible stories depending upon what is happening to him. Israel who wrestled with the mysterious being in the dark of night has a name which means 'the one who struggles with God', *yisra-el*. Interestingly, Superman's original father was called 'Jor-el' and the baby 'Kal-el'.

Certainly there is something very powerful in the Superman image and other religious metaphors are not too far away. Superman is saved from the destruction of his native planet by being launched into space in a rocket ship, the equivalent of Moses in his ark of bullrushes. He grows up as an adopted child, concealing his real identity from the outside world. He emerges when challenged by the realities of human injustice. From then on the legend takes its own course as this latterday Moses battles with his own version of Egyptian taskmasters.

Just to add to the imagery, someone observed that at least one part of his costume has special significance as well. His cloak rises out of his shoulders before hanging down – like the wings of a guardian angel, which is what he is in some sense as well.

I do not want to get carried away with these kinds of speculations. Essentially what I am trying to indicate is that our Jewish culture has become so open-ended in the West that it is almost impossible to be certain any more what it is at all, and what of Jewishness really is rooted in the Hebrew Bible. Moreover, how much of that connection to the Bible that we retain has come down to us directly through Jewish tradition and how much has come back to us secondhand, refracted through the prism of our post-Christian, Western culture. We have sold our ideas so successfully that it is hard to know any more what was once specifically ours, and what, if anything, remains uniquely ours today.

Jews have been part of Western culture and contributed enormously to it – especially in the centuries since the Emancipation. So much so that the Jewish contribution is synonymous with major influences and movements within the the Western world. I was once told a Jewish joke by a Muslim that seems to sum up the problem. He told me about the five wise Jews who changed the world. The first one said, 'it is all up here' (indicating the head) – and that was Moses. The second wise Jew said, 'no, it isn't up here (indicating the head), it's here! (indicating the heart) – and that was Jesus. Along came the third wise Jew and said, 'it isn't here (the head), and it isn't here (the heart), it's here! (indicating the belly) – and that was Marx. Then along came the fourth wise Jew and said, 'it isn't here (the head) and it isn't here (the heart) and it isn't here (the belly), it's here! (indicating the genital region) – and that was Freud. Then along came the fifth wise Jew and said 'it isn't here (the head) and it isn't here (the heart) and it isn't here (the belly), and it certainly isn't here (the genitals) – it's all relative! (Einstein). In the relative universe we inhabit our Jewishness runs across a broad continuum of expressions and appearances, and the Bible is but one small part of the source for some.

Roots for the future

In terms of the quest for Jewish identity we seem to have reached a point where it is extremely vague, and its relationship with the Hebrew Bible quite tenuous. In fact in the initial context of this talk I felt it necessary to turn the question inside out and suggest that the only legitimate way in which we could talk about the 'Biblical Roots of Jewish Identity' was to accept our own responsibility today to create them anew. I concluded in the following way:

> The Bible is a witness that the whole of our history was infused with a sense of religious vocation. We could exist in any number of social or political forms – as tribes, as a people, a nation, an

empire, a commonwealth, a community of refugees. But the constant factor throughout the thousand years of recorded biblical history was that ultimately we owed our identity to our faith in God. And this faith was expressed in very concrete terms with the covenant which allowed us to be subservient to the will of God without robbing us in any way of our human worth, authority and responsibility. In so far as the Bible records the struggle of individuals and the people as a whole to grasp the implications of this and live out the consequences, it offers us a way of refining our own experience and gaining encouragement for our own efforts.

Mirrored in the Bible are Israel's experience of struggle, defeat, destruction, exile, return and renewal. We find in it the guidance of laws and teachings, but also the great debate that our own prophets and thinkers have had about the workings of God in the world and our human understandings and misunderstandings of them. At the heart of scripture is an astonishing honesty and humility that always subsumes our individual and collective ego to something greater than us and beyond us. The Bible is based on the recognition that admitting the truth about our own failures and being willing to criticize ourselves are essential attitudes and actions for the progress and development of our people and of humanity as a whole. In today's world where so many of the old religious certainties have fallen away, the Bible provides a record of one people's attempt to understand its own experience of God in all its myriad forms. Moreover its very form of composition challenges us to enter into a dialogue with it and through it to the experience that brought it into existence.

In this sense the Hebrew Bible is not merely a history book indicating our origins and roots as a people or a religious community. Just as in the past it continues to create and shape Jewish existence whenever we open ourselves to it and accept the challenge it provides to us. Perhaps it is in this sense alone that we can talk with any certainty today about the Biblical Roots of Jewish Identity – they are our roots if we set about making them a fundamental part of our Jewish future.

On the relativity of exegesis

I am conscious that this has been a somewhat tortuous exercise. We have explored a particular inner Jewish concern and used the Hebrew Bible as a means for doing so, while at the same time stepping in and out of the exercise to look at the process itself. We have also admitted into the arena of biblical exegesis some less familiar participants, particularly novelists and psychoanalysts, whose insights often deserve greater attention. But in the end I am only reminding us that what Yeshayahu Leibowitz and Judith Plaskow have argued within the confines of the Jewish world applies as well to all religious traditions that concern themselves with the Hebrew Bible, and indeed to all who study it within a whole host of academic disciplines. We address our own particular community or communities with a shared set of presuppositions and in effect translate the symbolic language of the Hebrew Bible into a symbolic language of our own.

What I have tried to suggest is that there may be a way in which we can pay more attention to this relativity by means of a process of dialogue. Because another of my own presuppositions is that the Hebrew Bible by its very nature invites us into a dialogue with itself and how better to further that process than by working with each other in the same spirit.

Perhaps all I am doing is translating into a modern context some of the basic assumptions about the study of the Torah that informed the creators of the midrash. They suggested that 'there are seventy faces to Torah' (Alphabet of Rabbi Akiva). They recognized that though one could decide what a text might mean for certain purposes, for example in legal matters, it never lost its plain 'common sense' meaning (Shabbat 63a).[20] To paraphrase my teacher Rav Shmuel Sperber, 'exegesis provides an answer, but without removing the question'. Or to conclude with a more classical rabbinic source, when the Schools of Hillel and Shammai disagreed on a particular point, a heavenly voice proclaimed: '*eylu v'eylu divrei elohim hayyim*', 'Both these and these are the words of the living God!' (Erubin 13b, Gittin 6b).

The Bendorf Sermons

This section is a way of exploring the subversive nature of the Bible in a more public context. For those of you who dislike sermons I apologize – though you may take some heart from the fact that I also dislike them, whether delivering my own or listening to those of others. In fact they are awesomely difficult things to get right, as any practitioner will tell you. The context of a religious service raises unattainable expectations for some and grim resignation in others. A colleague tells against himself the story that the chairman of his synagogue slept consistently through his sermons. When the Rabbi once plucked up the courage to ask why, he was told: 'It's all right, Rabbi, I trust you.' The story has gone the rounds too much for me to believe that it really happened to the one who first claimed it as his own. Likewise this story told by another colleague as overheard in his own congregation. Before the end of his sermon one of the congregation left only to meet another latecomer coming in. 'Has Rabbi X finished his sermon?' asked the newcomer. 'Yes,' came the reply, 'but he's still talking.'

Given such odds it is a brave person who ventures to preach at all, let alone expose old sermons in print. But those that follow do seem to illustrate, albeit sometimes indirectly, some of the themes of this book. In fact they belong to a special context and have been important occasions in my life. For the best part of thirty years I have led an annual Jewish–Christian Bible Week and a Jewish –Christian–Muslim Student conference (JCM) at the Hedwig Dransfeld Haus in Bendorf, near Koblenz. I have retained the privilege of preaching the Shabbat morning sermon in the Jewish service. For the JCM conference, which takes place in the spring, I have usually taken the Torah reading (the parashah) of that week as a basis, and tried to relate it to the theme of the particular conference. However, as you will see, the readings in spring when it takes place are not always the easiest of materials to work with. Fortunately the Bible Week, which comes in the summer, offers many other Bible texts from the subject we have been studying that year as we have worked our way, so far, from Genesis to Ezekiel.

For me this sermon has been a way of testing out how far I am still in touch with what is going on in the conference itself beneath the surface and am able to offer something relevant to the needs of the people there, not excluding myself.

While I would start thinking about these sermons after the first few days of the conference they usually had to be composed within a forty-eight hour period so that they could be translated into German in time for the service. I would, and still do, go into a 'sermon mode' for that period, quite distracted from the daily events of the conference itself. Without access to other Jewish sources for inspiration I am forced each time to go deeper into the biblical text and 'read out' or 'read in' something appropriate for our context. Some of the ideas are more forced than others but I try to indicate where I am taking particular liberties with the text. This effort of imagination sometimes produced ideas that I was able to follow up later in a more scholarly manner.

Part of the subversive role of the Hebrew Bible is to challenge conventional ideas, and both of these conferences have set out to do that in their own way: deepening the dimensions of Jewish–Christian dialogue through a shared reading of the Hebrew Bible, or assaulting the layers of fear, suspicion and prejudice that exist between the three great monotheistic faiths.

Sermons are an odd literary form. The classic Rabbinic sermon will begin with an unusual verse, often taken from the prophetic reading for that Sabbath, a verse that is seemingly totally unrelated to the Torah reading. The preacher then leads the community through a series of ideas and associations till concluding, triumphantly, with a verse from the Torah portion of that day. I have rarely tried such an exercise and it does require an audience who know how the system operates. For Bendorf the problem is compounded by the fact that, particularly for the Jewish–Christian–Muslim conference, I cannot assume any prior knowledge of the Bible text at all. So enough background has to be given so that any subsequent remarks make sense.

The other problem with sermons for me is how to make a point, convey a message, without becoming too moralistic and putting everyone off, exhorting without exhausting. (I have tried, more or less successfully, to weed out the ones in which I fell into that

*particular trap!) Needless to say they also have to hold the attention.
As yet another old sermon joke has it: If you haven't struck oil in ten
minutes, stop boring!*

I have arranged the passages chronologically by the year of their
composition (JCM ones first, followed by the Bible Week examples)
rather than trying to follow the order of their appearance in the Bible.
I have also resisted the temptation to make more than minor
corrections.

7

Purity and Impurity –
Learning a Biblical Language

JCM 4.4.81 Parashat Tazria-Metzora (Lev. 12)

One of the strange things about the interfaith 'trialogue' between Jews, Christians and Muslims is the way that points of contact and areas of agreement keep shifting. Judaism, as the 'firstborn', shares elements with each of the other two even though they have diverged from each other. This sermon provides a good example. Judaism has moved a long way from the concepts of ritual purity contained in the Hebrew Bible, but many of the elements were nevertheless retained in Rabbinic thought and practice. Whereas for Western Christians, those most commonly represented at the Bendorf conferences, such matters have very little significance, they do remain important concepts for Muslims. So it was the latter who were most interested in this particular analysis.

The Torah reading for this week is one of the hardest in the Pentateuch to understand and one of the most difficult to preach on. One is tempted to quote the opening words of Leviticus 12, 'And the Eternal said to Moses . . .' and go off into a sermon about 'revelation' rather than try to tackle the actual contents. How does one talk about purity and impurity caused by childbirth, or the laws about some disease that may or may not be leprosy, in the context of a religious service? If one does try to approach it and not merely ignore it, the usual starting point is to examine it in its historical context, perhaps say a little bit about the Priestly code and then quietly drop it in favour of something more relevant. And yet I think we have a responsibility to look a little closer at the details of the text, despite their difficulties, and try to understand what is really going on beneath the surface. The reason for this is simply the importance attached to this material by the compilers of the Torah. The detailed analysis, the repeated warnings that breaking these laws could be disastrous for the community, that it may even be a matter of life or death, should make us want to understand what they are about. Clearly we are dealing here with a symbolic language, and though we no longer have access to it completely, we can begin to penetrate it and maybe learn something for ourselves.

Let us look at the opening section from Leviticus 12. If a woman gives birth she is *tamey*, 'unclean' or 'impure' for seven days. If it is a son, for the following thirty-three days she must remain away from the sanctuary and not touch anything which is set aside for cultic purposes. If she gives birth to a daughter that thirty-three days is doubled to sixty-six days. At the end of this time she brings an animal for a 'burnt-offering' and another for a 'sin-offering' to the priest who sacrifices them to God and thereby declares her *t'hora*, 'clean' or 'pure' again, and atonement is made for her. What is going on?

Let us first get rid of certain prejudices we may have about the text and its terminology. The word *tamey*, 'unclean' or 'impure' is not a pejorative term. It is not a word that makes any moral judgment about the person who is *tamey*. It does not mean 'dirty', 'bad' or anything else like that – it does not really mean 'unclean' or 'impure' as we conventionally use the words today. It is a purely ritual term meaning that such a person is not fit to enter the sanctuary because of some temporary state of physical disability or abnormality. Behind it lies a system that thinks in terms of 'wholeness' in a very physical way – God has created men and women in a certain state of perfection and in that state they are to come before God. If there is a discharge coming from the body, however temporary and however normal it may be, during that time one should not enter the innermost part of the sanctuary.

The whole system implies a consciousness of the holiness, otherness and power of God, that means that one does not approach God in a casual way. The rules, of course, do not only apply to women. A man who has a seminal emission is likewise *tamey* till the end of the day. And the discharges that come from either a man or a woman affect the things that they come into contact with. If a man's seed comes into contact with clothing, it can cause others who touch it to become *tamey* for the rest of the day – and if he has had intercourse with a woman, she is also *tamey* for the same period (Lev. 15.16–18). Conversely, a menstruating woman conveys *tum'ah* to anything she touches for seven days equivalent to the time of her period, and if, by mistake, she has intercourse with a man during this time, he too is *tamey* for seven days (Lev. 15.25).

It is interesting to note that the regulations distinguish between physiological discharges like these and pathological ones – these render men and women *tamey* till the condition clears up and there are even more stringent regulations to prevent them 'contaminating' anyone else by contact with things they touch. However normal bodily excretions like urine and faeces do not affect people in the same way, and perhaps we are dealing here with some concern with discharges relating to procreation as having special significance.

One other misunderstanding should also be cleared up at this point. The woman after childbirth brings a 'sin-offering', a *chatat*. This does not mean that she has sinned, or that sin has anything to do with the procedures here. She has been in a temporary state of exclusion from access to the sanctuary – now that she is allowed back in an appropriate offering marking the re-entry and re-acceptance into the normal community is required and that is the function of the *chatat* – and it is used for all situations that require such a re-entry and re-establishment of the ritual relationship with God.

There is one puzzle that remains in our text that is not so easy to explain – the discrepancy between the thirty-three days period for a boy and the sixty-six for a girl. I do not think that this reflects some concealed sexist attitude about the relative worth of male or female chidren – after all the exact same offerings are brought for the thanksgiving ceremony afterwards. Perhaps we have a clue in the regulations concerning a menstruating woman who sleeps with a man. He becomes *tamey* for seven days, as if he has become himself a menstruant. There are occasions when a newly-born baby girl will have a vaginal discharge or bleeding because she has been affected by the withdrawal of her mother's hormones so that in effect two 'women' have produced a discharge. So the mother has to take on the *tum'ah* of the baby who cannot act for herself, and the period is doubled.

Having discussed all this, it is legitimate to ask what relevance it has to us? Why bother to spend so much time on what is such a remote system. In Judaism the immediate relevance of all these laws disappeared with the destruction of the Temple, and the interesting idea was given that since we have no more the possibility of removing *tum'ah* at all, we are all, in this sense, ritually unclean, and the problem effectively no longer exists.

Let me suggest two points where it becomes important for us. Firstly there is an interesting phenomenon that arises out of the growth of women's movements in the world. I have seen liturgies composed by Jewish women that try to discover a religious expression for the significant events in their own life-cycle. Among these there is the attempt to create prayers and rituals related to the onset of menstruation. It is often assumed that such prayers are a new invention, but it is clear from what we have discussed that a consciousness of the religious significance of such events is very deeply embedded in the earliest strands of our biblical tradition and that perhaps a greater investigation of these materials would be helpful. But beyond that, such texts as these remind us of the importance of relating all aspects of our life, the most physical as well as the most spiritual, to God and, indeed, to the life of the community as a whole. Since we are discussing here menstruation and seminal discharges, it should be possible to extend such studies to the whole area of our sexuality in terms that are as objective and non-moralizing as the language used here.

Basically such passages remind us that we have a responsibility to give to our tradition the best of our attention, intellect and intuition, to take it seriously as far as we can in its own terms and not merely dismiss it because at first it seems remote or obscure. Eventually we might learn how to integrate its insights and perceptions into our lives. More than that, the very precision with which this material is presented should serve as a lesson. One of my teachers, Leslie Shepard, once pointed out how such laws considered things in the greatest of detail. Religion today has lost that precision and it can be found instead in areas like science. If we could only measure a religious truth with the same accuracy with which engineers measure microdimensions of time or space! The comparison is strange at first, but the challenge it presents is worth considering.

What is the importance of this passage for us here in this conference? Questions of purity and impurity, *tum'ah* or *taharah*, were not merely personal matters. They were things that affected the community as a whole, because if someone entered the sanctuary in an unfit state there could be terrible consequences for the whole community. As the closing verses of the entire section point out, the sanctuary is the place at the centre of the camp and of the community where God's presence was to be located. If we wish ourselves to enter that sanctuary, to take seriously our religious commitment, what we do has consequences for all religious communities.

As Jews we recognize that we have a mutual responsibility for each other. If a Jew does something well, not many people may notice it. But if a Jew does something wrong, the consequences affect us all and may harm us all. I am sure that similar awareness exists among Christians and Muslims as well. But what the passage may teach us is that beyond our loyalty and commitment to our own particular community, we share a mutual responsibility to each other. It is not just that we belong to our own group, but we belong to God's community and what we do affects the witness of God's will that all believers present to the world. And that witness begins with the way we regard each other, the cleanness or uncleanness of our treatment of each other, the purity or impurity of our relationship to each other. That is no longer a peripheral or marginal aspect of our religious task. In a pluralistic society it is the central value by which we shall be judged – for if those who claim to follow the one God cannot relate to each other then God's name is desecrated in public. We who seek to enter the tabernacle of God must try to purify ourselves, of our prejudices and our self-centredness, if we are to bring healing to our troubled world and not merely ally ourselves with the forces that lead to its destruction. Whether the language we use is that of purity or impurity, whether we think of physical or spiritual readiness, the challenge of our *parashah* is to remind us at all times that we should be fit to stand in the presence of God alongside all others of whatever faith community who wish to enter. To recognize the responsibility we have towards each other is the first, the hardest, but also the greatest step.

Some of the ideas contained in this sermon were derived from working with Rabbi Julia Neuberger on her Rabbinical dissertation.

8

Individual and Community

This Shabbat is a special one known as Shabbat Shekalim, the Sabbath of the Shekel. On it we remember the tradition that all Israelites would bring a half-shekel coin to the Temple each year to pay for its upkeep. The special biblical reading from Ex. 30.11–16 links the gift of the half-shekel to a census. The coins would be counted rather than the people, for treating them as numbers alone was to put them into great danger. As the text explains, unless such a system was adopted, a plague from God would break out upon them. So they are to give the half-shekel for their own protection, as a 'ransom for their soul'.

On another level this half-shekel is a form of poll-tax or head-tax, a way of acquiring necessary funds for the upkeep of the sanctuary. This being a patriarchal society it is all the adult males who were called to participate. But the fact that each had to pay the same sum was a way of stressing their equality. As the text says, the rich may not pay more and the poor may not pay less. All make an equal contribution to the Temple, and in that sense all are equal before God. However, as politicians discover from time to time, not everyone has the same income, and what means little for some means an unfair amount for others. The very attempt to bring equality may be the cause of inequality.

A similar paradox emerges on another occasion in the biblical narratives. When the tabernacle was erected in the wilderness, and sanctified by Moses, the leaders of all the tribes brought sacrifices to celebrate the occasion (Num. 7). The Bible records in precise detail how each tribe came on successive days, with their gold and silver and the animals for the sacrifice. Twelve times the identical list is repeated as each tribe brought the same items. Here was real equality between them. But since each tribe was made up of different numbers of people, it would have meant different things to each of them to bring the same amount. The larger the tribe, the easier it would be to find the same number of offerings and gifts; the smaller the tribe the greater the sacrifice for all. Unlike the case of the half-shekel where everyone made an equal contribution, here the size of your contribution would vary depending on the size of your tribe. It was not the individual but the collectivity that determined the offering you had to make.

This dual way of operating nicely illustrates the dual nature of Israelite identity. In one sense they were equal individuals, each assumed to be capable of providing the half-shekel that was his own responsibility; but at the same time each was part of a collectivity, ensuring that the group as a whole met their shared responsibilities. Both the individual and the group were given proper respect.

This dual nature of our identity, as individuals and as part of a larger whole, continues to find its expression in Jewish experience and thought. Perhaps the most obvious illustration is in one of the key prayers that we recite today in this service. The Amidah, the Standing Prayer, is a major statement of Jewish self-understanding and aspirations. It begins by linking us to our ancestors, Abraham, Isaac and Jacob, as a way of asserting our continuity with our past and the unbroken relationship we have with God. All of the verses speak in the first person plural: it is 'we' who together say this prayer. It is as a community that we stand before God, subsuming our individual will to the collective hopes of the whole Jewish people. In the thirteen blessings that follow in the weekday services, we speak of our needs – for understanding of God's will, for our desire to turn always to God and for forgiveness for all we have done that drives us away from God's presence. We pray for health for our people and for individuals that we know and for the blessing of fruitfulness for the whole earth.

Our national prayers are also strongly there as well: for an end of exile, for the restoration of Jerusalem, for the establishing of God's kingdom on earth. Though our individual requests may become selfish or destructive, we can purify them by submitting our private will to the collective needs of our people as a whole. Our desires become refined as we pass them through the perspective of our tradition.

But despite all this emphasis on the collectivity the individual is not forgotten. Before the Amidah begins we say quietly to ourselves a verse from the Psalms. 'O God, You open my lips then my mouth will declare Your praise' (Ps. 51.17). The reciting of all the blessings that follow is not a mechanical matter nor simply a collective task that requires no evaluation or commitment. I who stand before You have to be able to recite these petitions with confidence in their truth and trust that they indeed represent the will of God. I am challenged at the deepest level to recognize my individual responsibility for what I say.

At the end of the prayer comes another verse from the Psalms as a seal upon what we have said. 'May the words of my mouth and the meditation of my heart be acceptable to You, God, my rock and my redeemer' (Ps. 19.15). May there be integrity between what I think and feel within and what I say aloud. At the beginning we ask that God open our mouth, that we become a true channel for the word of God. At the end we reverse the relationship, we examine our own personal inner truth and pray that what comes from us ourselves will always be acceptable to God.

So the Amidah is at once the collective prayer of the Jewish people as a whole and our own individual affirmation of the values and beliefs that it contains. We are part of the collective and at the same time our own personal selves. We owe loyalty to both in equal measure. We must live with and respect the tension that follows from this our dual nature. We are therefore to be highly individualistic at the same moment that we are to be fiercely loyal to our people. But our loyalty to our people is measured by the degree to which we are prepared to maintain our independence of the collective, to criticize it, to go our own way. Loyalty cannot mean simple acquiescence because that would itself destroy our integrity as a people.

Perhaps in the same way our independence as the Jewish people is what we offer to the wider world around us. Our integrity as a people is tested in the greater collectivity of the nations and faiths of the world. As a people we too must be highly individualistic but at the same moment fiercely loyal to the collectivity of the peoples of the earth. That tension also is built into our existence as the Jewish people.

Let us return to the half-shekel with which we began. Why half a shekel and not a whole one? We need to find a partner so that together we can make a complete gift. None of us can build and maintain a Temple for God alone. We can only do half of the job

with what we have and what we are. That is the limit that is set on
our individuality. But that joining together is the bridge to our
collective identity as well. We share with another or we are less than
whole. We match each other, gift for gift, need for need, or what we
do remains incomplete. We have to recognize our partners in the
enterprise of building and maintaining a place for God in the world.

That is part of why we are here as Jews seeking our personal
matching half-shekels within our own people. But today it is not
enough to remain within the closed confines of our people alone. As
we learn every moment in a conference like this, everyone, from
every people and faith that is here, has brought their own half-
shekel. Alone we can none of us do the work of building the
sanctuary. We must each respect our individual community but
acknowledge that we belong to a greater community as well.
However difficult and painful it may be to accept responsibility for
the greater whole, that is the task that is placed before us.

As the text of Shabbat Shekalim warns us: If we also want to be
counted before God we have to bring our half-shekel with us. That
is the only way to save ourselves from the plague that threatens to
destroy us all. The issue is no different now from what it was when
the Temple still was standing. The offering we each of us bring, the
half-shekel we are willing to match with that of the other, is the
ransom we must pay for our very souls.

9

Religion and War

JCM 16.3.96 Vayakhel-Pekudey (Ex. 35.1–40.38)

The theme of this Jewish–Christian–Muslim conference was 'The Impact of War on our Religious Traditions', the choice being very much influenced by the events in Boznia, and indeed any number of recent wars where religious and ethnic issues were involved. The Hebrew Bible acknowledges the reality of war and offers some rules of conduct that are forerunners of the Geneva Convention (Deut. 20.1–20; 21; 10–14). Starting from the parashah *of that particular Shabbat I had to do some very fancy footwork to address the theme. But such a challenge can bring surprising insights. In my mind were clearly the kind of religious fanaticism that led to Muslim suicide bombers and the religious Jew who assassinated Prime Minister Rabin of Israel.*

This Shabbat two sections of the Torah are linked together, *vahakhel-pekudey*, and with them we complete the Book of Exodus. They are a strange series of chapters because they repeat word for word much of what has already appeared, the instructions about the building of the tabernacle in the wilderness, together with all its furnishing and the clothing of the priest (compare Ex. 25.3–7 with 35.5–9). It is a decidedly strange way to end a book that has begun in such an exciting and triumphant manner – with the enslavement of the Israelites, the birth and calling of Moses, the plagues, the Exodus from Egypt, the encounter with God at Sinai, the establishment of the covenant, the first great sin, of the golden calf, and the message of God's forgiveness.

Perhaps it was felt that after all this excitement we needed a pause to get our bearings, a time for consolidation. Perhaps Moses realized that what was needed now was some common task, something to which all the people could contribute. After the

destructive inner struggles that had taken place because of the
episode of the golden calf it was a time for sharing and healing. A
common project was a way of repairing the damage. Once again the
people were to offer precious items for a common religious
purpose, as they had for the golden calf, but this time for something
sanctioned by God.

The people clearly needed a concrete symbol of the presence of
their God. They had just come out of Egypt where such monuments
and symbols abounded. But if such a thing is to be built, it should be
done under controlled circumstances. The religious urge, the desire
to serve God, to make sacrifices, could so easily become perverted
into making an idol, something that resembled the divine but was
really a distortion of the religious ideal.

So Moses passes on the instructions, that all those whose heart
moved them to make an offering to God were invited to do so. For
the second time the Bible gives us the exact list of what materials
they were to bring:

> gold, silver and bronze; blue and purple and scarlet stuff and fine
> twined linen; goat's hair, tanned rams' skins, and goatskins;
> acacia wood, oil for the light, spices for the anointing oil and for
> the fragrant incense, and onyx stones and stones for setting for
> the ephod and for the breastplate (Ex. 35.6–9).

At this point I want to step back from the biblical text itself and
address a question to it. Jewish tradition suggests that whatever the
problems that we are facing at a given time, whatever the issues that
are in the air, somewhere within the weekly Torah reading there is
something that will address them. So I found myself asking what
could be found within this week's reading that would be helpful in
considering the subject we have been discussing, 'the impact of war
on our religious traditions'.

My first response was less than completely serious. Whatever our
views about the effect that our holy scriptures have on our conduct,
I think I can safely say that nothing in this particular text has ever
encouraged someone to make war, commit a violent act or behave
in anything but an exemplary fashion. Since there is not enough
information given in this section actually to enable anyone to build
the tabernacle, there is literally nothing you can do with this text –
except read it, puzzle over it and wonder why so much space is
devoted to it, not only once but twice.

To this latter question I have no answer. So instead I focussed on the materials used for the building and realized that there was something here that might be appropriate. Gold and silver are symbols of the greed and wealth that can lead people to war. But the Bible itself takes this further. When King Solomon was at the height of his powers he built an armoury known as the House of the Forest. In it he placed two hundred shields of beaten gold (I Kings 10.16). When his son Rehoboam was defeated in battle by the King of Egypt, the shields were taken away as tribute, and replaced by Rehoboam with shields of bronze – the third metal on our list (I Kings 14.26–27). The beautiful colours, the blue, purple and scarlet could be the colours of the flags we fly to promote our national identity and emphasize our differences from others. The goat-skins and ram-skins are the usual covering of shields; the acacia wood might otherwise have been used to make spears. The oil that is used for anointing is the symbol of leadership and power and plays a role in the inner biblical civil wars to establish the true king. The stones for the ephod were used to determine whether it was a propitious time to go to war or not. The stones for the breastplate, worn by the high priest, can remind us that the priest had a special role to play in war – and clergy have always been called in to bless armies and weapons.

If we follow this line of thought we can see that all the elements of warfare, those that cause and those that are used to fight it, have their place in this tabernacle dedicated to God, where God's presence is to be found. So perhaps we can see here the heart of the religious dilemma. If religion is to concern itself with all aspects of human activity, all human emotions, it cannot ignore the passions and actions that lead to war and take place in war. To exclude religion is to suggest that it has nothing to say to this central human dilemma. Worse, it is to give up the struggle for human progress before we even begin. To incorporate these symbols in the tabernacle is a way of seeking to transform them, to domesticate them, to tame them, to bring them within our control so that they cease to be destructive forces. But therein lies the risk that their power and attraction in turn pervert our religious forms and actions, the tabernacle becomes again a golden calf. We have taken the struggle into the religious realm, but the struggle does not change simply because we put it into there. Rather it can become even more potent if we do not take full responsibility for what we do with it.

And let us be under no illusions about the seductiveness of war or its paradoxical achievements. War is the most destructive but at the some time most creative of human activities. Look at the extraordinary outpouring of human imagination that goes into the improving of weapon systems. The radar that makes it safe to fly a plane is a product of war. The miniaturization that gives us our walkmans and CD players and our computers would never have developed without the threat or experience of war. Without the two World Wars the opportunities for women in the work-place may never have developed. There is a very deep level in which we experience benefits from war, until we come later to count the cost – the coherence it gives to society and life; the sense of solidarity amongst us; each moment together becomes precious, each parting sweeter and sadder, when we do not know if we will meet again; it is a time for some when we feel truly alive, when life has a purpose, when complexities and moral uncertainties can be set aside, for we know with absolute clarity who is our friend and who our enemy, who is good and who is bad. In the right circumstances, none of us is immune from the attractions or seductiveness of violence and war. That is also part of the inner struggle with our evil inclination that is central to the religious approach to life.

Religion is about taming these passions, transforming them into service and acts of love. But that is why it can go terribly wrong. Religion rides the tiger of human emotions, passions, desires, lusts, fantasies, greed. It can conquer them or be overwhelmed by them. The war that happens outside in the world is the war that begins within our souls.

Our chapters complete the Book of Exodus. It began with slavery and ends with the risk of another kind of slavery. It knows the risks of creating another golden calf, yet still asks us to give freely for a religious purpose. The gold and silver and bronze, the blue and purple and scarlet, the skins and wood and oil and stones are the materials that each of us has in our hands. And each of us can choose how to use them – for violence or for peace, to build the emotions and weapons of war or to construct a tabernacle to house the presence of God.

10

Imagining Moses

Bible Week 27.7.73 (Exodus)

The following sermon must have been one of the first I ever gave in Bendorf, some two years after being ordained as a Rabbi. I was still experimenting with a rather dramatic style, sometimes attempting to enter the mind of a biblical character, and fascinated by existential journeys and rhetorical questions! In defence I must point out that, my youth apart, we were still trying to discover and understand the unique quality of this Jewish–Christian Bible Week in Germany where Jews and Germans were attempting to meet despite the horrors of the past. And I was personally struggling to define for myself my own approach to the Hebrew Bible, knowing only how dissatisfied I was with so much of contemporary scholarship.

This evening I want to ask a question that has become of great significance during this Bible Week. Why do we read the Bible?

Is it out of antiquarian interest in old legends? Philology? Or because we have to teach to others and want to improve our knowledge of the text? Or because we are searching for truth, for revelation, for the hand of God? Perhaps it is because in our time, when it is hard to find God, we read the stories about those people for whom God was a real experience.

Through their stories, we learn our own story – as a person, as a member of the group into which we are born, as a member of the society in which we grow up, and of the world around us.

We have studied this week the Exodus, and already examined in passing something of the story of Moses. Perhaps we can turn again to him now, and try to piece together our own story, how we see what happened.

It was a lonely road through the desert, and he had time to think of the events that led him there.

He remembered his mother – a shadowy figure, a face from his childhood that he lost when he entered the palace in which he was to grow up. And with that figure mysterious stories, suggestions of another family somewhere. So that as he grew to manhood, to success and rank in the palace, he knew all the time that he had a secret. That he was in some way different. That he was a stranger in the home in which he grew up.

He remembered the taskmaster, with the whip in his hand and the body of the Hebrew slave at his feet. The blow he struck in anger. That moment when he knew that with this blow he had lost forever his adopted home. He had killed a part of himself, and there was no way back, even if he tried to bury the secret in the sands of Egypt.

He remembered those strange Hebrew slaves who stood about him. Those ugly people, those angry, bitter people – who were his people. He offered them his love – and they rejected him. He offered them his life – and they betrayed him.

And a man with no home, who had lost his childhood, and destroyed his way back to the place in which he grew, was left alone to wander the desert.

But life is not always so dramatic, and he found a new home. Because there is always someone who will love him, and need him and want him, somewhere in a distant land. A stranger again. Loved and in safety. A father, a shepherd.

How many times did he visit the mountain of God before he saw the bush? How many times did he see it burning, before he understood what it meant? How many times did he approach and withdraw because he knew and dreaded what it would mean?

Forty years he waited. Until he was a man past new beginnings. Until he was safe from new adventures. Till he could come to the mountain without fear – to ask about his death; to make peace with his life.

The command was the one he feared – go back to the family you left behind. They need you.

'But who am I? Who am I to go?'

'I will be with you.'

'Who shall I say sent me?'

'I cannot be named as you would try to name Me.'

'But they will not believe me.'

'Why do you malign them whom you do not know? And anyway, you have a task to perform.'

So Moses returned to perform his task. What will be his end? He will be buried in an unknown grave. What will be his reward? He will be called 'the faithful servant'.

Why do we read the Bible?

11

David Dances

Bible Week 1.8.81

*This sermon is rather long by Bendorf standards, and you may
need to re-read the relevant stories of King David to understand it.
But the riddle of David's power, the tension between sexuality and
spirituality, are important subjects to address, and show the Bible
at its most subversive in its depiction of its heroes.*

I want to start today not with the *parashah* but with the texts we
have been studying this week. In chapter 3 (of II Samuel) we read
about Rizpah, the concubine of Saul, who is rumoured to be taken
by Avner (the late King Saul's commander-in-chief). Whether this
is true or not we are not told. Nor is it clear whether this is merely an
affair of the heart or part of Avner's strategy to show his control of
the throne. Certainly he uses it to show the power he has over the
weak Ishboshet (Saul's son and successor) so that Rizpah is reduced
to a mere pawn in a power struggle.

The same chapter introduces us again to Michal, David's first
wife, who becomes the price David exacts from Avner as evidence
of his good faith. As Saul's daughter she is a potential step on
David's path to the throne – and we have no idea from the text
directly as to whether David cares for her or not. She was, after all,
his first wife and on one occasion defied her father to save him. But
her fate has been bound up in the struggle between David and Saul.
Her personal history has been so disturbed with her forced marriage
to Paltiel, that she too emerges as someone tossed around by the
warring factions. Her individual worth and life is forgotten in the
transactions that go on around her. Perhaps it is important to note
that not only women suffer this way in the stories before us. One of
the most significant comments on the events is made by the narrator
in depicting poor Paltiel walking weeping beside his wife on her way

to Hebron (back to King David) and then being dismissed by Avner
– another toy in the hands of kings working out their public destinies
and private vendettas.

But the juxtaposition in the same chapter of the stories about
Rizpah and Michal points to another idea. Both of them are in the
personal household of the respective kings, and the ultimate test of
the power or weakness of a man is his ability to defend his
household. Ishboshet is too weak to guard Rizpah and also to keep
Michal and must yield her to David; David has the power to take
Michal, whether he personally wants her or not.

The stories about Michal reach their climax in another episode
and it is the implications of this I wish to examine a little bit further.
I refer, of course, to chapter six where David attempts to bring the
Ark into Jerusalem. This episode, and particularly Michal's angry
taunting of David, seems to have aroused considerable discussion in
the study groups and one can easily understand why this is so. It is
one of the most human and personal texts in our chapter, the one
with which we can most easily identify and where there is both a
deep mystery about the power and will of God, and also the
responses of the human heart.

There are many ways we can read Michal's behaviour. She and
David have grown apart in the years during which they have been
forcibly separated. There stands between them still the ghost of
Saul, and perhaps her insistence on the dignity of the king is an
expression of her concern about the dignity that should also be
afforded to the daughter of the king. And were we to read the story
as marriage guidance counsellors we would quickly find ourselves
wondering about the state of sexual relations between the two of
them that leads her to interpret David's dancing before the Ark as a
mere sexual display before the women of Jerusalem. In fact the
closing observation that she had no children comes to us as no
surprise.

But I want to move beyond the view of David that Michal could
see peeping out of her window, to a closer look at the man himself
on this day of perhaps his greatest achievement. For David has had
a great religious success that day. Not in the fact of bringing the Ark
to Jerusalem, but because of the way he reacted to the mysterious
event that happened on the way. Uzzah grasped the Ark and died
suddenly. David is angry at God for spoiling the magnificent
procession. And then, with a moment of clear perception, David

learns the mystery of the Ark that the sons of Eli (I Sam. 4) never understood. That it is not his private possession or magic symbol, but that it is God's; that the true relationship to it is not that of ownership but of awe and fear. And with this comes an insight of his own unworthiness to use the Ark at all. In a moment David's universe has been turned inside out. In the centre is no longer the hero of many battles, the successfully anointed king of the two parts of Israel – but instead there is God. And it is because of this first act of *teshuvah*, 'returning', 'repentance', by David, this turning about, that he is allowed to take the Ark the rest of the way. It is no longer subsumed to his ambition, but his ambition, at least for this moment, is subsumed to the will of God.

And then comes Michal. And the success on the religious plane is made bitter by the failure on the human one. But Michal's criticism of the dancing David, no less than God's, is based on a deeper insight into the motives and power of the king. For Michal has rightly pointed to the sexual energy that is part of this enormously complex man.

Paradoxically in the ecstasy of this moment of entry into Jerusalem, that sexual drive has been channeled into a deep religious awareness and joy. She has only judged by outer appearances. But the parallels to these two episodes show the potential for tragedy that still underly them: for the warning about the Ark will reach fulfilment in God's refusal to allow David to build the Temple. And the accusation of Michal will come to fruition in the story of Bathsheba. Michal looking down from her window is trapped inside the frame, she remains outside of life, looking on, looking down, on David below. By not taking the chance of moving beyond her limited view, she never enters his life or her own, and childless she dies. David, too, looked down on Bathsheba and took the risk of going down to her.

And at the moment when he must choose what to do with that energy she has evoked, he makes the wrong decision. He cannot sustain the self-control that might yet transmute that drive into other channels. He abuses the responsibility that belongs to his power – the energy that led him from the sheep-folds to the kingdom; the energy that flowed into poetry and song; the energy that sprang into his dance. So the hideous train of events begins, ending in murder and the tragic history of his sons. But with it begins also the enormous work of return, of redeeming himself, of unmaking what he can, of living with the consequences. A royal sin needs a royal repentance. The greater the man, the Rabbis teach, the greater within him is the *yetzer*, the drive that can express itself in ambition or sexuality, or evil, the drive that it is our task to master.

And sometimes the choice is very clear – this is potential for ourselves, for our ego, or it can be for God. At times we dance for the handmaids, at times for God. This is not a moralistic position – it speaks of a choice with consequence either way. What is important may not even be the choice at all, but only the realization of the extent of the drama that unfolds around it, of what is at stake. And beyond even that the mystery of *teshuvah*, of return. We are not David – we are ourselves. But how do we learn, except, as David, by the bitterness of making the tragic mistake?

The David we have met this week is still the David of legend. True there is violence around him, true he is hard to find behind the political schemer, the manipulator. But he has made one major turn in the matter of the Ark. And his greatest challenge is ahead of him. How strange that the tradition sets alongside his triumph as a king, his founding of an empire, the simple story of his temptation and fall and the painful journey back – but then it is the journey of David's soul that earns him a place in our lives.

12

Disciple

When we read the Elijah and Elisha stories in sequence we are struck by their many similarities. Both prophets announce a drought (I Kings 17.1; II Kings 8.1); both provide food for a widow through miraculous means (I Kings 17.8–16; II Kings 4.1–7); both bring a boy back to life (I Kings 17.17–24; II Kings 4.8–37); both, together or singly, part the waters of the Jordan (II Kings 2.8–14).

There are even linguistic formulations that they share. The 'hand of God' comes on both of them (I Kings 18.46; II Kings 3.15). Both are surrounded by horses and chariots of fire (II Kings 2.11; II Kings 6; 17). When both are on the verge of death or translation into heaven, someone exclaims 'My father, my father, the chariots of Israel and their riders' – Elisha says it of Elijah (II Kings 2.12) and Joash, King of Israel says it of Elisha when he is dying (II Kings 13.14). Both adopt a special crouching posture (the unusual verb *gahar*) when they try to bring about a miraculous event – Elijah when praying for rain (I Kings 18.42); Elisha when bringing the boy back to life (II Kings 4.34). Both use the same oath formula about their relationship to God: 'As the Eternal God of hosts lives before whom I stand' (I Kings 18.15; II Kings 3.14; 5.16).

In short we are persuaded of the similarity of the two figures on all sorts of dimensions. Elisha is very firmly established as Elijah's successor. There are, of course, also differences. Both are zealous for God, though Elijah is perhaps more precipitate, more urgent and demanding – even forcing God to follow his extreme line. The struggle between Elijah and God is indeed part of the drama of the stories, far more than in the case of Elisha. Elijah remains a solitary figure against a stark desert landscape, with rare periods of relationship with others. Elisha is more often seen with his disciples and against a human landscape. His anger is also there and his contempt for the secular authorities he must struggle against. He too can conjure up destructive or healing powers but somehow remains a more approachable human being.

The stories about the two prophets and the very language used sketch two characters who share similar powers and a common task, yet who remain differentiated individuals. What was their relationship?

Elijah meets Elisha at the lowest ebb of his prophetic career. His great success at Mt Carmel is past (when he defeated the prophets of Baal), and he is on the run from a vengeful Queen Jezebel. In despair he complains that all the people are untrue to God and that only he remains as a prophet (I Kings 19.10). In answer God seems to remove the burden from him and asks him to anoint Elisha in his place. When Elisha asks him to return home to say farewell to his parents Elijah tells him to 'go back' – the same terms used by God when dismissing Elijah from his prophetic task. Perhaps we can see here in Elijah's response a hint of something other than concern for his young successor. For Elijah is to be replaced. His sense of defeat has been accepted and perhaps in that there emerges an anger and resentment against the one who takes his place.

But what of Elisha? We assume he is still a young man. He has the mantle of Elijah cast over him and gives up all that he has to follow his new master, the man of God. He becomes his servant and disciple; as the text expresses it: 'he poured water on the hands of Elijah' (II Kings 3.11).

But discipleship is no easy matter. For to serve a spiritual master is also to serve a human one. It is to learn the secrets and foibles and anachronisms of the master. In matters spiritual it is to feel the inadequacies of one's own religious commitment and perception. In matters human it is to undertake the daily chores of the master, to set aside one's own desires and needs for the sake of the other. Yet the two aspects are not to be divided. For learning to serve, to put one's own ego at the service of another, is the inner secret of discipleship. The disciple hands over his private will and desires into the hands of the master. It is a surrender, but one in which his own need for self-respect and personal integrity are still present, let alone his own greeds and jealousies, needs and weaknesses. The disciple desires to obtain the qualities of the master. He would not recognize them if he did not already have access to them within himself. It is in the interaction with the master that he comes to release them, cultivate them, let them grow time and again beyond his current limited understanding. But always there are the temptations to make short cuts, the risk of becoming too knowing about the inner life of the spirit merely because of his relationship to the master. And here lies the other great problem. For the pride of the pupil will be met by the corrective insight of the master – whether expressed aloud or merely conveyed by the glance that says: 'You are not yet there and deep down you know it.' So a part of the disciple's pain is the shame he feels at his own mistakes, a pain he may only be able to express in resentment and even hatred of his master. The master is the one who guides and at the same time the one who seems to stand in the way.

One day the disciple must leave and make his own way in the world. It is hard to make the break for he is too much made in the mould of his master, too much fashioned by him – at least so it seems from outside. Elisha adopts the tasks and repeats the actions of Elijah. Yet he is also unique and must trust the insights and experience that are his. And at times the direction he takes will lead him away from the understanding and path of his master. It is at the point of separation that both are severely tested. The master must know when to let go and trust both what he has taught and his intuition that made him choose the disciple in the first place. A Rabbinic view says that the teacher must pull with one hand and push with the other – lest he push the pupil away or pull him too hard in his own direction. That was the mistake, the Rabbis taught, that Elisha made with Gehazi. That was also the mistake made by the teachers of Jesus in the view of a passage censored out of the Talmud. The master too is fallible and tested.

But the disciple is also tested in the way he leaves his master, especially when he has begun to find his own path. The disciple who stays too long may hate the master who stands in the way of his own independent growth. The master who cannot let go may try to destroy the pupil who is now his potential rival. Spiritual power or authority is never a guarantee against the simplest of human weaknesses. Indeed the greater the power the greater the destruction that can be unleashed. Holy wars are bitter and cruel.

I have tried to look at this struggle between master and disciple without sentimentality. It is one of the great spiritual paths and it has broad implications. It happens when any religious figure has a following and tries to pass on what he or she has learnt. But beyond that it is also a model for the relationship between spiritual movements and the sects that break away from them, even between two great world faiths like Judaism and Christianity that bear such an ambiguous relationship to each other. Whether the model is one of master and disciple, or parent and child, the same struggle exists: to gain acceptance by the master as a true successor, yet respect for an independent path that may lead in new directions. And such a struggle cannot be described solely in terms of friendship or tolerance. It is inevitably a struggle between love and hate, envy and rivalry. It is a battle for power and control as well as mutual respect and wonder. There is no peace that is not earned by an inner recognition of where the real battle must be fought.

Yet all too often we fight in the outer world when the real struggle is within. For if the inner battle is not recognized for what it is and tackled with all the seriousness it requires, then we will fight it in the outer world and risk destroying everything in the process. All intense relationships, parents and children, husband and wife, master and disciple, are miniature enactments of that struggle at the heart of our spiritual striving to meet God. And maybe the deep misgivings, ambiguities and mistrust at the heart of the Jewish –Christian relationship is the arena in which we have to face our own inner call and journey.

Does Elijah leave Elisha at the right moment for both? Does Elijah regret his parting or recognize a new journey, a new task for his urgent, zealous nature? Does Elisha insist on accompanying so as to gain the last piece of his master's power, or is he frightened to make the final break and become in turn the new master to a troubled group of disciples and nation? And what pain did they inflict upon each other and what miracles did they achieve in the many years they shared with each other? The biblical record is incomplete. But as must happen to every generation of master and disciple, of teacher and pupil, both crossed the Jordan together but one returned to face the world quite alone.

13

Jeremiah Revisited

Bible Week 25.7.92 (Jeremiah)

I do not know what sparked off this meditation. I wonder also what the congregation in Bendorf thought of it since most of the time they must have sat there guessing when I would get to some kind of recognizable subject related to our studies of the prophet Jeremiah. But then that is half the fun of a sermon – provided you can sustain interest and curiosity till you get to the point, and always assuming there is a point you can reach! But flippancy apart, it is one of the effects of the Bible Week that it can inspire this kind of outpouring that feels 'right' for the Week and for me at that time.

There is too much information. Data impinges upon our eyes, ears, nose, mouth, skin. Our senses are constantly bombarded with stimuli. There is so much input that it threatens to overwhelm us, so we block it out selectively. We do not see all that there is to see, nor hear all that there is to hear. Through the cacophany of a crowded street, a child will hear the chimes of an ice-cream van, a mother will identify the cry of her child. The rest is pushed away, rejected, by invisible mechanisms of which we have almost no conscious awareness.

The whole surface area of our skin is alive to receive information. Every muscle and joint in our body records the tone and tension that it is experiencing. Every heartbeat sends its messages to centres that control our posture, our balance, our movement. Glandular secretions circulate in our blood, responding to short term stress or sustained effort, competing, balancing each other out. And each of these actions and reactions in turn feeds its information to higher centres that re-assess our position in space, our respiration, the discharge or holding back of electric pulses, the onset of a myriad minute chemical transactions. Yet all of these responses, these millions of units of information that we monitor every moment of our lives, remain silent, unnoticed, automatic.

Were we ever to become conscious of even one small part of them, we would be deafened by their roaring, drowned in their insistent call for our attention. So much information that is essential to our life itself is invisible, indeed repressed, for our own self-protection. We survive only because we are selective in what information we register, acknowledge and allow to invade our consciousness. We have within us a hierarchy of awareness, whereby the higher control, accepts or suppresses the lower.

Our inner world has a richness we can never fully experience. But what we receive from the outer world is also subject to censorship by conscious and unconscious parts of our mind. Everything we see or hear or smell or taste or feel is registered and acknowledged or ignored. A myriad of pieces of information compete with each other to be noticed, and here too we have a hierarchy of controls to filter out what we cannot allow to reach us and affect us. There is indeed an entire commercial industry dedicated to breaking through our defences, to finding the potent images that demand that we notice them and respond.

So our life is spent collecting fragments of information, from without and from within, through our senses and our emotions, through our reason and our intuition. From these fragments we compose a narrative, a logic, a thread of coherence and consistency that helps us define at any time who we are, and helps determine how we handle the next bundle of information that comes our way. We create the story that is our life, accept into it what we can accept and reject what we have to reject.

If we are this selective with information that is neutral and valueless, that may ultimately be only a distraction, what happens to information that operates on the level of values? How do we handle data that challenges or questions what we take for granted, that seeks to insinuate itself into the very hierarchy that sustains our private or collective identity? What cannot be tolerated simply cannot be heard – it is too dangerous for the organism, so it is suppressed, relayed down to a lower level of organization, to a place where it does not impose itself or cause trouble. In the structure of our consciousness it takes on the nature of an itch or sting. They too are warning signals of damage done to the organism, but the body knows that they are not life-threatening so need not yet be taken too seriously. They are monitored, their presence is felt, but their impact can be overridden, their message drowned in activity or by concentrating on other things – in the knowledge that in time the impulses will cease to register, the nerves no longer react, the threat will simply go away.

Complex though we are, we too are but a part of a larger whole. Beyond our individual selves are the groups to which we belong and their further organization right the way up to the most complex structure of our society. And the same rules of selective perception seem to apply the higher up the scale of collectivity that we go. The lower is subordinate to the higher and the higher preserves its identity and security by its selective suppression of the information that comes to it from below. The totality of its existence can be sustained because it can afford to ignore 'x' amount of pain among its individual members, 'y' amount of unrest, 'z' amount of criticism. Only so much information can be taken in and processed, only so much can be allowed to affect the operation of the whole. There may be nothing malign in this, no conspiracy to suppress or harm, merely the contrasting forces of effectiveness and inertia, together with the sheer weight of convention and convenience, of self-interest and self-protection and survival. Nevertheless at a critical point the sheer weight of new data may break through, from within the organism or without. Then the higher levels go into shock, realign and readjust, shift the balances, discard the old, accommodate the new – and the process begins again.

There is little room for a wild card in the game. A virus in the body, a question that nags the individual, a prophet who cannot accept the complacency and certainties of those who hold power – all are equally dangerous. As an itch they can be tolerated, ignored, perhaps rationalized away. But if they become a threat to a higher level, then they must be stopped – for the sake of the organism as a whole, acting out of its own understanding of where danger lies. So the words of prophets are suppressed, and they are put under house arrest, or imprisoned or killed and the organism breathes easily again.

Yet prophets still arise. Driven men and women who filter out from reality a different vision, who hear in the tumult of the world the cry of pain. And because they hear and see what others cannot hear or see, they are condemned to a lonely struggle on the margins of their society or on the verge of madness.

Jeremiah fought the deadening effect of the hierarchies of his own society: the cult that replaced an openness to the word of God with an empty piety – *heichal adonay, heichal adonay, heichal adonay*, 'the Temple of the Eternal, the Temple of the Eternal, the Temple of the Eternal' (7.4); the desire for peace, without addressing the prerequisites of justice and responsibility – *shalom, shalom v'eyn shalom*, 'peace, peace, but there is no peace' (8.11); the love of the land that could become another form of idolatry – *eretz, eretz, aretz*, 'the land, the land, the land!' (22.29). The organism as a whole could not tolerate what he had to say and condemned him. Then the new reality that Jeremiah foresaw broke through and the old world was destroyed. But the record of his words, his struggle and his life were preserved.

The human organism lives on through history. The weight of convention and commonsense holds us securely in place; the inner and outer hierarchies maintain their checks and balances; they give us the illusion of safety. But Jeremiah still calls us to see what we do not want to see and hear what we do not want to hear. Having spent time in his company, he is now a part of us, a fragment of the story we tell about ourselves. And it may just be that through us he will continue to trouble the world.

14

Young Jeremiah

Bible Week 24.7.93

This was the third year we had studied Jeremiah and I was clearly feeling the need to lighten up the atmosphere a bit. It is also no accident that, as Principal of a Rabbinic seminary, I was preoccupied with some internal issues as well. Would a Jeremiah ever have got through our own three-day admissions procedure at Leo Baeck College? On a more serious note, it is important to remember that the prophets were not wild individuals who suddenly appeared in the market place calling for doom and destruction. They belonged to something like a guild and underwent a training in their craft. (Jeremiah claimed he was only an 'apprentice' (a 'lad') when he was first summoned by God (Jer. 1.6).) But out of their ranks stepped some exceptional figures who could not simply say yes to the wishes of the king or flatter the desires of those in power. They were doomed to tell the truth as they saw it.

I had better make it clear that what follows is a parody, including all the pseudo-scientific stuff at the beginning – people do not always spot it and can get quite upset! (In fact I got the giggles part way through delivering this sermon and never recovered.) But being a parody does not make it any the less serious.

This particular chapter allows me to end this book by writing about one of the most subversive figures in the Hebrew Bible. Certainly Jeremiah was seen as such in his time, and the retention of his book allows him still to speak and challenge. But his 'subversiveness' is also paradoxical, as befits the prophetic word that is always conditional on people's behaviour. Before the destruction he was the most passionate critic of his society; after the destruction his was the voice of comfort and consolation.

The world of biblical scholarship has been enriched by the finds in the caves of Qumran. However a number of documents were not made available to the scholarly world for very many years. Inevitably this has led to the suspicion that some important materials were being suppressed and it is very gratifying that the full texts have now been published. Nevertheless there remains one groups of documents that have only recently become available. What follows is the first public presentation of these materials and it is very appropriate that this should happen here during the twenty-fifth Jewish–Christian Bible Week.

The documents in question seem to be the records of one of the Prophetic Colleges that functioned during the seventh and sixth centuries BCE prior to the destruction of Jerusalem by the Babylonian army. They include the files that were kept on a number of candidates for prophetic office, recording the results of their preliminary interviews, their progress through their studies until their final anointing as prophets, together with some closing remarks. These records are of enormous importance since they belong to that rare group of materials which give extra-biblical information on people named in the Bible. It is particularly fortunate that among the names recorded is that of Yirmiyahu ben Hilkiah whom we can only assume is the same Jeremiah of Anatot we have been studying this week.

The Document begins with what seems to have been a considerable debate about his eligibility for the prophetic office.

He presented himself at an unusually young age, claiming that he felt that he had been called to the office of prophet even before he was born, that God had indeed chosen him while still in the womb. The members of the Admissions Board were inclined to overlook this youthful conceit, assuming that the rather shy and retiring young man had somehow identified himself with the stories about the birth of Samson. However, since many find it difficult to express their vocation in a straightforward way the Board felt that there was something refreshing in his directness. Since it was not expressed in a boastful way, but rather modestly and even with a sense of bewilderment and anxiety, it was decided to take him at his word and not pursue this particular matter further.

The record shows that he came from a priestly family though it was noted that his branch had been removed from their regular place in the Jerusalem Temple as a result of a variety of inner political struggles that the Board did not wish to go into. Suffice it to

say that he came from the ranks of the best Jerusalem families and
should under normal circumstances have been guaranteed a place at
Beth Yeshayahu, Isaiah College, the seminary established almost a
century before by former students of the great prophet of Jerusalem.

But in the event things did not turn out to be so straightforward.
The major difficulties were raised by Achav ben Kolayah (Jer.
29.21) who seems to have prepared a psychological report on the
young man as part of the admissions process. We have on record
only the notes of his findings, but one can see how damning they
could have been for his chances of admittance to prophetic training.

Achav noted a rather autocratic streak in young Jeremiah, that
reflected at the same time a serious disrespect for authority figures.
One must assume that Jeremiah did not show to Achav himself the
respect that he might have expected so we may have to treat
Achav's judgment in this particular matter with a degree of caution.
However we should take seriously the following remarks that were
clearly the result of talking with people who knew the young
Jeremiah over a period of time. It seems that he was subject to
mood swings that at times were so severe that, in another society, he
might have been hospitalized for clinical depression. In such
phases, it seems, he felt that others were talking about him, he
became abusive to family and friends alike, accusing them of
plotting against him. Sometimes, during the worst phases of his
illness, he became so aggressive that he even provoked the kind of
behaviour against him about which he complained.

A third factor was considered to be particularly important. Achav
noted that though already in his twenties the young man refused to
follow the normal procedures of seeking out for himself a wife.
When quizzed on the matter, he shrugged it off on the grounds that
he felt that his vocation demanded that he remain single – a
suggestion that Achav found disturbing in the extreme. The true
prophet, he argued, needed to have a stable and secure home life,
and should have the responsibility of a wife and family to give him
an appropriate sense of duty and caution in all his dealings. After all
it was only someone who was aware of the broad political and social
realities who could effectively serve the state in the important role
of Prophet. Moreover, Achav argued, an unmarried prophet did
not make a good role model. The great Isaiah, who was after all the
founder of this College, had used both his wife and children as
symbols in some of his most memorable prophetic utterances. It

would be dangerous to call into question this central Israelite value, the blessing of having children, and certainly when it came from one in direct prophetic line from their founder!

Achav's report is not yet completed, and what follows gives a good insight into the sort of skills and indeed personality that were being sought at that time for the prophetic office. Achav felt that Jeremiah had a somewhat abrasive personality. He was sensitive, but only with regard to his own feelings, which were easily hurt – the feelings of others did not seem to concern him so much. Achav summed up his report with the warning that the young man had poor communication skills and would have great difficulties holding down a job in a small village community. Unless the College was able to find some post that played to his strengths, particularly his strong sense of faith, Achav felt that it would be wrong to take him on and expend so much money on training someone who would be unable to function effectively.

In the ensuing discussion a number of points were made. In Jeremiah's favour was the fact that he was well connected at court through his family. Someone on the Board suggested that all personal considerations apart, it was important to remember that funding of the College came out of the royal coffers – a wrong word to the king from Jeremiah's family might prevent the building of the new wing to be named after the Queen mother. Though such material considerations should not play a part when the religious future of a young man was under consideration, such practicalities were nevertheless important.

Perhaps it is no surprise that the member of the Board who raised the strongest objections was none other than Chananiah ben Azur, who was to have a serious disagreement with Jeremiah in later years and, indeed, at the cost of his life. His objection, however, was on purely academic grounds. Young Jeremiah was illiterate! Now he might be an intelligent young man, and it was understandable that living in a little village like Anatot his education had been neglected, but the reputation of the College had to be considered. How could one know that he was even capable of the serious scholarly courses he would have to undertake? And anyway, unless he had a photographic memory, how could he keep a record of all the various things he would have to learn? These objections might have proved decisive in keeping Jeremiah out, but the Head of the College, at the time Micah the Morashite, still functioning as chairperson in his ninety-fifth year, pointed out that he had had a private discussion with Jeremiah's father and they had agreed that Jeremiah could employ a scribe to take notes for him. In fact, as soon as Jeremiah was accepted, Baruch ben Neriah would be offered the job.

The decisive voice in accepting Jeremiah came from a senior member of the faculty, Huldah the Prophetess. Somewhat to the surprise of the Board, she began by accepting all their reservations about the young man. His mental instability, his isolation, even his tendency to fanaticism, were very worrying. Would it be right, she asked, to give such a person the undoubted power that went with the prophetic office? And yet, she said, was that the only issue that we had to consider? Was our task as prophets merely to make people comfortable? Was it not rather the case that we were all isolated, detached from our society, so that we could better serve God? What had impressed her about the young man was his acute sense of justice, his unwillingness to compromise on things that he considered important. Part of that could be put down to his youth and in time he would doubtless mature. She felt that he needed to get out of the rather narrow society of Anatot for a while and get a broader experience of the world. Since it was important to test out his academic skills, perhaps he could go to Babylon to brush up his Aramaic there and get to see what big city life was really like. It was possible that he might even wish to stay there and give up his idea of studying to become a Prophet. It seems that she said this with a rather ironic intention, but it may have been taken seriously by his tutors at a later stage since he clearly had contacts with Babylon in later life.

But her concluding remarks were much more serious. There were clearly hard times ahead. The world was changing about them. New political powers were emerging and one could not be sure what would happen to current alliances. In such a time one needed many different kinds of Prophet to be able to bring the word of God to the people in fresh ways. Perhaps a touch of anarchy, of passion, even if it meant stepping on a lot of toes, was essential for such a period. Jeremiah might not be the Prophet for quiet times, but for the storms that might lie ahead his love for God and his love for Israel might just provide the voice that was needed. And who knows, perhaps when all the rest of their current favourite students had long been forgotten, a creative, difficult, slightly crazy figure like Jeremiah might still be remembered.

Probably as a result of Huldah's words, Jeremiah was accepted.

As might have been predicted his journey through the College was stormy. There are at least two occasions noted when someone felt he should be expelled – once for leading the students on a protest march to a new Babylonian shrine that was erected just outside Jerusalem, and once for insulting Achav who had the misfortune of being appointed his tutor. He got high marks for preaching, though his teacher thought he rather overdid it with some of his symbolic actions. Apparently he would wear outlandish clothes for a few weeks and then bury them somewhere and parade the rotten bits about in Jerusalem. Nevertheless he got a distinction for his paper on the failure of Josiah's Reform, and despite his personal isolation, he had a large attendance whenever he gave a seminar. He gained a reputation throughout the country for his work on the contemporary application of covenant law.

We might have assumed that after the conflicts of his first years as a student he would have completed his course with relative calm. But half-way through the anointing ceremony in the Temple he stormed out complaining that the money wasted on the forty bullocks they had slaughtered would have been better used paying welfare to war widows.

The file is closed with a comment from a different hand – presumably the successor of Micah as Head of the College. It is possible that the writer was Uriah ben Shemaiah who got into trouble in later years, fled to Egypt and was deported and eventually killed by the king for prophesying in treasonable manner in wartime (Jer. 26.20–23). Jeremiah nearly fell foul of the same law himself so perhaps we can see in this judgment on his College career the voice of someone who influenced the young Jeremiah in his formative years. The text reads:

In closing this file we remain convinced that it was right to train Jeremiah at Beth Yeshayahu. He is a gifted young man with a strong sense of vocation, and if he can ever find the right niche for his obvious qualities he should be very successful. Unfortunately, given the current rather conservative political climate, I can see little future for him in Jerusalem. I can imagine only one situation when his great gifts would be needed. But that would be a time of such overwhelming disaster for Jerusalem and indeed for the entire nation that I hope and pray that he is never called upon to speak the words of the One True God.

Notes

1. The Subversive Bible

1. Michael Walzer, *Exodus and Revolution*, Basic Books, New York 1985, pp.ix, 4–6.

2. Perhaps this self-imposed limitation leads to the second occasion when God 'consults' before taking an action – in coming down to confuse the languages at the Tower of Babel (Gen. 11). In one reading this is a response to the human activities of the building of the tower, but it can also be seen as a further stage in the experiment, creating distance between the various human groups and separating them geographically to see what comes out of this.

3. See my *Bible Lives*, SCM Press 1992, pp.76–79.

4. For a detailed study of irony the book *Irony in the Old Testament* by Edwin M. Good, SPCK 1965, reprinted 1981 by Almond Press, Sheffield, is the classic text. A more recent study is *On Humour and the Comic in the Hebrew Bible* ed Yehuda T. Radday and Athalya Brenner, Almond Press 1990.

5. See my *Form and Meaning: Studies in Literary Techniques in the Book of Jonah*, Almond Press 1983 and *Bibles Lives*, pp.134–48.

2. Abraham and Justice

A version of this chapter was given at a 'Trialog-Tagung in Cologne on 1 December 1992 under the title 'Tradition and Interpretation of Abraham, from the beginning till today: "Abraham eint – Abraham scheidet"'.

1. Erich Fromm, *You Shall Be As Gods: A Radical Interpretation of the Old Testament and its Traditions*, Fawcett Books, Greenwich, Conn. 1966, p.25.

2. *Aggadat Bereshit* 25 qoted in Israel Isaac Hasidah, *Ishe Ha-Tenakh*, Reuben Mass, Jerusalem 1964, p.17.

3. For a more detailed study of the cycle of Abraham stories see my *Bible Lives*, pp.23–32.

4. Shalom Spiegel, *The Last Trial*, Schocken Books, New York 1969, pp. 20–21.

5. For a summary and critique of these views and other pyschoanalytic material see Silvano Arieti, *Abraham and the Contemporary Mind*, Basic Books, New York 1981.

6. Amir Gilboa, 'Isaac' from *The Penguin Book of Hebrew Verse*, edited and translated by T. Carmi, Penguin Books 1982, p.560.

7. Shin Shalom, 'Ishmael my brother' quoted in *Forms of Prayer for Jewish Worship Vol. III: Prayers for the High Holydays*, Reform Synagogues of Great Britian 1985, p.891.

8. From *Tanna de be Eliyahu* (Lublin edition, 1897), cited respectively as 'end ch. 20 and p.48' in *A Rabbinic Anthology* ed C.G. Montefiore and H. Loewe, Meridian Books and The Jewish Publication Society of America, New York and Philadelphia 1963, p.557.

3. *Exodus and Liberation*

1. Joseph B. Soloveitchik, *Reflections of the Rav (Lessons in Jewish Thought adapted from Lectures of Rabbi Joseph B. Soloveitchik by Abraham R. Besdin)*, Jerusalem 1979, p.199.

2. Erich Fromm, *You Shall Be As Gods*, pp.36–37.

4. *The 'Chosen People' and the Peoples*

This chapter is in part based on an article 'The Attitude Towards Egypt in the Book of Exodus' published in Concilium *6, 1988, pp.11–20, and in part on a lecture 'The Relationship to the People and the Peoples in the Scriptures in Judaism' given at a conference under the title 'Religion und Nation' at the Evangelische Akademie, Berlin–Brandenburg, 24–26 November 1995.*

1. In Magonet, *Bible Lives*, pp.57–58.

2. N.M. Sarna, *Exploring Exodus: The Heritage of Biblical Israel*, New York 1987, pp.58–59.

3. R.E. Clements, 'goy' in G. Johannes Botterweck and Helmer Ringgren (eds), *A Theological Dictionary of the Old Testament* Vol. II, Eerdmans, Grand Rapids 1977, pp.426–30.

4. Martin Buber, *Biblical Humanism: Eighteen Studies by Martin Buber* ed Nahum N. Glatzer, Macdonald 1968, p.86.

5. There are critical questions about the composition of this text, but I will treat it in the final form as it appears in the Hebrew Bible.

6. William G. Braude and Israel J. Kapstein, *Pesikta De-Rab Kahana*, The Littman Library of Jewish Civilization, Routledge 1975, p.256.

7. Reuven Hammer, *Sifre: A Tannaitic Commentary on the Book of Deuteronomy*, Yale University Press 1986, pp.217f.

8. The Rabbinic concept of the seven commandments given to the sons of Noah follows this general idea. There are certain basic human values and any individual or people that abides by them are certain of a place in the world to come. They contain several prohibitions, including idolatry, sexual misconduct and murder, and the positive command to establish a system of justice.

5. The Book of Jonah and the Day of Atonement

This chapter is based on an article that appeared in SIDIC *(Service International de Documentation Judeo-Chretienne), Vol. XVIII, No. 3, 1985, pp.4–8. I wrote it in Rome during the filming of the movie* King David, *which I described in* A Rabbi's Bible *(SCM Press 1991, pp.73–85). I dedicated it at the time, perhaps a little tongue-in-cheek, to the producer Marty Elfand, the director Bruce Beresford and the star Richard Gere. Though the movie opened and closed within a week in Los Angeles and, it seemed, did not fare much better elsewhere, it was a bold if flawed attempt to bring the Bible to life in another medium.*

1. For a fuller study of Balaam, see my *Bible Lives*, pp.67–76.

6. The Biblical Roots of Jewish Identity

Published as 'The Biblical Roots of Jewish Identity: Exploring the Relativity of Exegesis', JSOT 54, June 1992, pp.3–24.

1. There are few systematic introductions to the mediaeval Jewish commentators in English and not all of their commentaries have been translated. Good introductions to the subject are Louis Jacobs, *Jewish Biblical Exegesis*, Behrman House, Inc, New York 1973 and the invaluable five-volume work of Nehama Leibowitz, *Studies in Bereshit (Genesis); Shemot (Exodus); Vayikra (Leviticus); Bamidbar (Numbers); Devarim (Deuteronomy)*, translated and adapted from the Hebrew by Aryeh Newman and published by The World Zionist Organization, Department for Torah Education and Culture in the Diaspora, Jerusalem 1980. The following are some of the individual commentaries available in English:

Rashi (acronym for Rabbi Solomon ben Isaac), 1040–1105, who lived in France, the most influential Jewish commentator of the Middle Ages. His commentary on the Pentateuch accompanied the first printed edition of the Hebrew Bible, *Pentateuch with Rashi's Commentary*, translated into English and annotated by Revd M. Rosenbaum and Dr A.M. Silbermann, Shapiro Valentine and Co, London 1946;

Abraham Ibn Ezra, 1089–1140, Spanish born Rabbi, philosopher, grammarian and Bible commentator who travelled extensively in North Africa and Europe: *The Commentary of Ibn Ezra on Isaiah*, translated by

M. Friedlander, London 1873, reprinted by Philipp Feldheim Inc, New York. See also Friedlander's *Essays on the Writings of Abraham Ibn Ezra,* Publications of the Society of Hebrew Literature, London 1877 and also *The Commentary of Abraham Ibn Ezra on the Pentateuch. Vol. 3. Leviticus* translated by Jay F. Shachter, Ktav Publishing House, New Jersey 1986;

Radak, Rabbi David Kimhi, *c.*1160 – *c.*1235, grammarian and Bible commentator in Provence: *The Commentary of Rabbi David Kimhi on Psalms CXX–CL,* edited and translated by Joshua Baker and Ernest W. Nicholson, Cambridge 1973;

Nahmanides (Moses ben Nahman, Ramban), 1194–1270, Spanish mystic, philosopher and physician. His commentary on the Pentateuch is translated by Charles B. Chavel, *Ramban (Nachmanides) Commentary on the Torah,* 5 vols, Shilo Publishing House Inc, New York 1971. See also *Judaism on Trial: Jewish–Christian Disputations in the Middle Ages,* edited and translated by Hyam Maccoby, The Littman Library of Jewish Civilization, Rutherford, Madison, Teaneck, London and Fairleigh Dickinson University Press, Toronto 1982;

Obadiah ben Jacob Sforno, *c.*1470–*c.*1550, Italian physician, philosopher and Bible commentator, teacher of Johannes Reuchlin; see *Sforno: Commentary on the Torah,* translation and explanatory notes by Rabbi Raphael Pelcovitz ,The ArtScroll Mesorah Series, Mesorah Publications Ltd, New York 1989;

Unfortunately there are as yet no translations of Shadal (acrononym for Samuel David Luzzatto), 1800–1865, Italian scholar, philosopher and Bible commentator, director of the rabbinical seminary in Padua. In his Hebrew commentary on the Pentateuch and Isaiah he is the first to enter into debate with modern biblical scholarship.

2. For a bibliography of Nehama Leibowitz see note 1. Incidentally, she is the sister of Professor Yeshayahu Leibowitz cited elsewhere in this chapter. An evaluation of her work can be found in Yaira Amit, 'Some Thoughts on the Work and Method of Nehama Leibowitz' in *Immanuel: A Journal of Religious Thought and Research in Israel,* No.20, Spring 1986, pp.7–13.

3. For a Jewish critique of the impact of Christian typology on Jewish Christian relations see Geoffrey Wigoder, 'A Jewish Reaction to the "Notes"' in *Immanuel: A Journal of Religious Thought and Research in Israel,* No. 20, Spring 1986, pp.67–83, 77. For recent studies on how typology might be understood in different ways today, see *SIDIC*, Vol. XXI, No.3, 1988. The English edition is entitled 'Problems of Typology: Reading the Jewish and the Christian Scriptures' and includes articles by Francesco Rossi de Gasperis, 'Christian Typology: Is it still valid? If so, which typology?', pp.4–8; Francesca Cocchini, 'The Fathers of the Church: Some Aspects of the Typological Method which are valid today', pp.9–11; Carmine Di Sante, 'The "Old" and the "New" Covenant: How to Relate the Two Testaments', pp.12–17.

4. Yeshayahu Leibowitz, 'An Interpretation of the Jewish Religion' in *Judaism Crisis Survival: An Anthology of Lectures* ed Ann Rose, World Union of Jewish Students, Paris 1966, pp.33–34.

5. Judith Plaskow, *Standing Again at Sinai: Judaism from a Feminist Perspective*, HarperCollins, New York 1991, pp.20–21.

6. For more on the perils of being technical adviser on a biblical film see ch.6 of my *A Rabbi's Bible*.

7. This exegetical principle was particularly developed by Nahmanides in his commentary on the Pentateuch; e.g. on Genesis 12.6 he asserts it as a general principle for understanding the stories of all the patriarchs.

8. Sigmund Freud, *Moses and Montheism*, Vintage Books, New York 1959.

9. Marthe Robert, *From Oedipus to Moses*, Anchor Books, Doubleday, Garden City, New York 1976.

10. Given the large number of Jews involved in different forms of psychoanalysis and psychotherapy, surprisingly few have explored biblical themes. One of the most sympathetic and consistent of such studies is that of Erich Fromm, *You Shall Be As Gods: A Radical Interpretation of the Old Testament and its Tradition,* Fawcett Publications, Greenwich, Conn. 1966. Stemming from the Jungian tradition, but working with the Hebrew text, are two studies by Rivkah Schärf Kluger: *Satan in the Old Testament*, Northwestern University Press, Evanston 1967 and *Psyche and Bible,* Spring Publications, Zurich 1974. For some recent applications of psychotherapeutic insights to biblical materials see the issue of *European Judaism* (Vol. 22, No.2, Winter 89/Spring 90, Issue 43) on the theme of 'The Therapist and the Bible'.

11. Dan Jacobson, *The Rape of Tamar,* Penguin Books 1970.

12. Stefan Heym, *The King David Report,* Quartet Books 1977.

13. For those who prefer a more 'old-fashioned' novel about David, I would strongly recommend Charles E. Israel's *Rizpah*, Macmillan 1961.

14. Stefan Zweig, *Jeremiah (a Drama in 9 Scenes),* Leipzig 1917; ET Thomas Seltzer, New York 1922.

15. Stefan Zweig, *The World of Yesterday*, Cassell 1943, p.194.

16. Franz Werfel, *Hearken to the Voice*, Jarrolds 1938.

17. Franz Kafka, *The Trial*, Penguin Books 1953.

18. For a study of the biblical themes that have been taken up in literary form, see Sol Liptzin, *Biblical Themes in World Literature*, Ktav Publishing House, New Jersey 1985.

19. Harlan Ellison, 'I'm looking for Kadak' in *Approaching Oblivion* (New American Library), reprinted in *The Illustrated Harlan Ellison*, Byron Preiss Visual Publications, New York, n.d.

20. For a recent study on the 'plain' (*peshat*) and 'applied' (*derash*) meaning of the text see David Weiss Halivni, *Peshat and Derash: Plain and Applied Meaning in Rabbinic Exegesis*, Oxford University Press 1991.

Index of Biblical References